FALL IN AND CHEER

By the same author:

THE KUMQUAT STATEMENT:
Anarchy in the Groves of Academe

By John R. Coyne, Jr. and Patricia Coyne:

THE BIG BREAKUP:
Energy in Crisis

FALL IN AND CHEER

by John R. Coyne, Jr.

DOUBLEDAY & COMPANY, INC.
Garden City, New York
1979

ISBN: 0-385-11119-3
Library of Congress Catalog Card Number 78-7751

Printed in the United States of America
First Edition

To my mother and father,
and to
Pat, Jennifer, John, Amanda, and Charity.

That the politicians are permitted to carry on the same old type of disgraceful campaign from year to year is as insulting to the people as would be a gang of thieves coming back to a town they had robbed, staging a parade, and inviting citizens to fall in and cheer.

—Edgar Watson Howe 1853-1937

CHAPTER ONE

IT was a good year for nostalgia, albeit nostalgia of a somewhat peculiar variety. There was Richard Nixon, for instance, doing the Frost interviews. Those of us who worked for Nixon, especially during the last days, always felt that he had scored a major public-relations triumph whenever he managed to display a few recognizably human traits on television. And that, in several of the Frost show segments, is precisely what he managed to do.

But what was most important, what evoked that peculiar nostalgia, was the context—or, more precisely, for most viewers, the lack of context. There was Nixon, looking just the same, spitting out those hard words—"punk" for Ellsberg, "trash" for Woodstein—which sounded particularly harsh, punctuating as they did what was ostensibly a chat between two men in an overstuffed room. But the problem was one of context. For most viewers it no longer exists, if it ever did. But it was there for Richard Nixon. Indeed, he has carried it to Casa Pacifica with him, where it shapes the days of his exile, surely one of the most unusual exiles in political history. That context is the decade of the sixties, and that is where Richard Nixon will always live.

That decade is fading rapidly, much faster than those of us whose lives were deeply touched by its excesses would ever have dreamed possible. Today, there's a sense of something lost, something that we all once tacitly understood but now can't quite satisfactorily define. Many of us became profoundly political during the sixties, and we stood on sharply etched, opposing sides. But that is over now, and the political and ideological positions of the sixties—the issues of that decade—seem already nearly as anachronistic as silver-standard populism or anarchism.

We no longer quite fit. Today a new political synthesis struggles to be born. Jimmy Carter, at least in 1977, seemed to have managed to take the thesis, the radical left politics of the sixties and early seventies, combine it with the antithesis, which was the conservative counterreaction that we liked to call the New American Majority, and synthesize the two in a way that was at least partially acceptable to some of those who stood at the two extremes, as well as to most of those who stood somewhere near the middle.

We don't quite like that, of course, those of us who were politicized during the past decade. There is, we tend to believe, a specific set of what we call "issues" that must be addressed in an ideologically acceptable fashion, the proper positions on those "issues" having been forged in the heat of the sixties.

Carter refuses to take those identifiable positions that fit within the context of the past decade, however. Thus, we call him inconsistent, evasive. He contradicts himself, we say. He waffles. During the campaign of 1976, for instance, he told us he opposed busing and abortion, two of those clear-cut "issues," and this made a number of conservatives happy. But he also said he was against constitutional amendments to outlaw busing and abortions, and this pacified many liberals. And he said it all in a very moderate way, thus pleasing moderates.

Inconsistent, we'd say later, when we put it all together. Just another two-faced—or three-faced—politician, we'd say, and attack him for his blatant inconsistency.

And of course, within the context we've established for the discussion of those issues, he is indeed inconsistent. But that is because our definition of consistency depends upon the acceptance of certain positions on certain issues, which we continue to define as we defined them a decade ago. In the meantime, however, Carter seems to have redefined consistency, and suddenly we find ourselves, frequently against our wills, dancing to his definitions.

Consider, for instance, his positions on energy and the neutron bomb, each of which manages to irritate both conservatives and liberals. There is no consistency here for those of us who hold clearly defined ideological positions. But Carter seems uninterested in pleasing us. Instead, apparently, he is intent on searching out the American political center, never an easy task. During the past decade, the Right spent much of its time insisting that the center was moving rightward, the Left that it was moving in that direction. And at both extremes the argument continues, although with much less conviction these days. Carter, however, was the first of the new-breed politicians to realize that we were all both right and wrong. In some ways we did indeed move right—or more specifically, back—toward the old values that we seemed to have mislaid. But in otherways, especially in matters of social welfare, we have continued to move left. Civil libertarian extremists may see signs of regression in such esoteric areas as homosexual rights or state-financed abortions. But the very fact that we seriously discuss something like the freedom to practice sodomy as a constitutional "right" says something about how far we have moved. And the direction in which that movement will continue to carry us is quite clear.

In matters of domestic social policy, we are heading steadily left, and Carter will do nothing to reverse that direction. True, he once promised us a balanced budget, the prospect of which is still so bewitching to conservatives that Barry Goldwater has promised to nominate Carter at the 1980 Republican Convention if he does so. But he also promised us, for instance, a comprehensive system of national health insurance, and although it will take a few years, we can be certain that if the economy allows it he will carry out that promise. When we get it, we'll no doubt wish we had back what we gave up to get it, as has been the case in nearly every nation that has socialized its health care system. But by then it will be too late, and if that's what a majority among us want, then that's what we should get. Sooner or later Carter will also attempt to give us such things as that long-discussed consumer protection agency, and eventually we can be sure that he will attempt to federalize such programs as welfare.

These trends do not make conservatives happy, yet even though they're suspicious, they respond positively when he plays the profound old chords. During the campaign, he spoke of values—of goodness, of decency, of morality, of the family, of love of God—and those of us who became rightist counter-revolutionaries during the period when all those values were so heavily under assault were deeply affected.

For us, more than anything else, the assault upon traditional values was what the sixties was all about. I remember, for instance, a significant moment in my own politicization at Berkeley when I listened to a tired professor of contemporary literature who seemed, in his comments, to epitomize everything that was going wrong with us.

"Principles and values make us unhappy . . . religion, nationalism makes us unhappy," he said. "Take care of matter and spirit will take care of itself. . . .The only reality is the reality of loneliness. Man is trapped in a prison house of self-consciousness, living in a metaphysical isolation. . . . Life is dirty and vulgar, all bestiality and human cannibalism. There is no authority in life or nature. . . . Man is guilty of the general crime of being alive."

This was a typical sixties lecture from a typical campus shaper of youthful minds, an unexamined series of careless observations growing out of an intellectual pastiche of Marxism, Darwinism, Freudianism, and Existentialism that passed for thought in the classrooms of the period—and perhaps still does, for all I know.

Such assaults on traditional values played a central role in the shaping of the context of the sixties, as students at campuses like Berkeley, encouraged by intellectual fashion, threw off those values that their professors, most of whom led quintessentially middle-class lives off campus, in the classrooms sneeringly called "middle-class." It would be somewhat sophistic, of course to attempt to draw a direct line from such professors to the Weatherpeople. There are a number of lines, some of them intersecting, others fading out. But that one line is nevertheless there, sometimes wavering, sometimes faint, but running in a fairly straight course.

The professor's observations just quoted, and others like them, formed much of the basic classroom currency of the age. And it had an effect. If you put a group of children from conventional families into what seems to them to be a highly intellectual atmosphere, and then you devote yourself to assailing, to making fun of, those conventional attitudes they bring from their conventional homes, chances are you'll make those children, many of them, ashamed to admit that they ever took those conventional attitudes seriously.

The trouble is, however, that those conventional attitudes are nothing less than the mundane codification of all the basic ideas and values that structure our society. Assail those ideas and values, discredit them, and unless the student possesses singular intelligence and character, he will turn his back on them. And when that happens, something must replace them, for people—and especially young people—can't survive as hollow constructs, without values and beliefs. Thus, in the sixties, many students who found a traditional system of beliefs in rubble around their feet ended by embracing the most popular and powerful set of beliefs available to them. And thus, in large part, was the New Left and the context of the sixties created, a context that was to give us Nixon and Agnew before it was destroyed.

We can, to a significant extent, thank the professors. Some of them, Herbert Marcuse, for instance, were active indoctrinators. But more frequently, the culprits were members of a conforming generation of professors who, through their fashionable parroting of the anti-"middle class values" line, helped lay the groundwork for the radicalization of a generation of students. And in the sixties, when their radicalized students turned on them, perceiving that these professors for the most part lived lives totally unrelated to the ideas they passed on, the professors were totally bewildered, simply incapable of making the connection.

This, in part, was what the sixties were about. And just as these men were hollow, so too were the institutions in which they worked. The sixties were also the last golden days of the computer deans and administrators who fervently believed that everyone and everything could finally be boiled down to one punched card. Class assignments were computerized, grades were computerized, billings were computerized, students were computerized. These were the days of apparently limitless supplies of federal money, when the favorite administrative one liner was, "As long as you're up, get me a grant." And the only thing the money didn't buy was a first-rate education, especially for overenrolled and undertaught undergraduates.

These were the days when, in a major public address, Clark Kerr could compare students to white rats. These were the days of the growth of structures for their own sake, run by men without centers. And it was this condition, more than anything else, that finally drove Mario Savio and the founders of the Free Speech Movement at Berkeley to throw their bodies on the machine of the university and bring it to a halt. That is precisely what they did, and as the decade progressed, increasingly radicalized students came to view the university as a microcosm of the society at large.

The university had grown into the multiversity, a tightly centralized, computerized factory, and as it grew, it lost touch with its primary constituents, the students. It commanded, forcing its constituents into computerized molds and seldom consulting them on matters of policy that directly touched their daily lives. And like the university, the megagovernment in Washington increasingly functioned in the same way. Once we were asked what we wanted. In the sixties we were told what we needed.

On the campuses, the excesses of the sixties in large part grew out of debased, eclectic, popularized, liberal theories about man, his society, and his education. In Washington, where the government, like the university, was discovered to be a similarly empty structure, much of the problem was the unconscious acceptance of popularized liberal political and philosophical theories, theories that were demonstrated to be bankrupt in the uproar over the war in Vietnam.

In the end, the Vietnam War was to prove as significant in its effects on the nation as World War II. The Second World War was the great unifying experience of the century. It brought us together as never before and laid the basis for the technological explosion of the next two decades. It also hurried the process of the redefinition of the relationship between government and the governed. The common good became the operative phrase, and we grew accustomed to giving up various small individual and economic freedoms in its name. The executive branch ate steadily into the power and prerogatives of the legislative branch, and anyone who protested was labeled a mossback by such academic architects of the imperial presidency as Arthur Schlesinger, Jr.

That presidency reached its culmination at the beginning of the Vietnam decade, when a young liberal President led us off on our last great imperialist adventure, to the applause of liberal Democratic technocrats such as Robert McNamara. And it began to unravel just a few years later. Somewhere along the line, perhaps when LBJ began bombing everything that moved, many liberals who had long advocated centralization came suddenly to understand precisely what was wrong with that tightly centralized executive branch controlled by an imperial President—it was no longer responsive, and that all-powerful President could turn out to be a bad man. And finally, in 1973, toward the end of the Nixon administration, liberal advocates of executive power finally discovered the beauty of those checks and balances of which they had previously been so contemptuous.

What was happening in Washington had happened on the campuses. Tightly centralized governments, like tightly centralized university administrations, must by definition treat their citizens as members of a great collective rather than as an assortment of individuals. And once a society is sufficiently collectivized, individualism is by definition undesirable, and those who govern inevitably lose contact with the individual citizens they ostensibly represent. Centralization means insensitivity, and it took Vietnam to make most of us realize this. But in the early days on the campuses, when the Free Speech Movement was founded, this had already become clear, and the war on the administrations of those campuses was microcosmic of the larger war that developed toward the end of the decade, the first great battle of which was fought in the streets of Chicago in 1968. The liberal technocrats and interventionists who had taken control of our government were strikingly similar to the new-breed administrators who controlled the campuses—in many cases, the same men—and the protests against these men quite naturally developed into protests against the men who ran the government in Washington. Men like Clark Kerr were the first surrogate figures for the President of the United States. The deans and administrators represented the cabinet members; the faculty, the members of the House and Senate.

At first, many of us who were later to turn right, to become counterrevolutionaries, found much to sympathize with in the protests of groups like the Free Speech Movement. We agreed that the campuses were corrupt, and we also believed that the government in Washington had grown increasingly unresponsive and unrepresentative. But at about the point where the Free Speech Movement became the New Left, we were forced to part company. There were many obvious reasons. Those of us who grew up in the fifties and served in the Armed Forces had at bottom a feeling for the country and its institutions that was, to put it simplistically, traditionally patriotic. We too believed that the universities and the government had lost their centers, had become empty structures run by hollow men. But in the end, we believed that the answer was not to demolish the structures—the logical end of the New Left philosophy, in its final stages personified by the Weatherpeople—but to put back in control of the structures men who represented democratic values.

And that is one of the reasons so many of us became partisans of Spiro Agnew. He was the man who said the things we had been waiting to hear. Nor was it just incipient members of the new American Right who saw him in this way. Toward the end of his tenure, he had become friendly with a number of the members of the Eastern intellectual establishment it had delighted him to pummel—among them Irving Kristol, Daniel Boorstin, *Commentary* writers, Harvard professors. James Reston referred to Agnew as the personification of "the old American verities," and out on the Coast, the old-line liberal academic S. I. Hayakawa, whose refusal to surrender his campus had led many, mistakenly, to view him as a conservative, was one of Agnew's strongest admirers.

On the afternoon of Agnew's resignation, before the news had gone out, I was asked to call Hayakawa and give him the news in advance. "I still think the world of him," said Hayakawa.

In many ways, the New Left and the New Right grew from similar sources. In 1964, when the Free Speech Movement was born, the Goldwaterites were asking, in similar ways, for many of the same things—more responsive government, more involvement in decision making, more recognition of the worth of the individual citizen. And in many ways, the development of the New Left concept of participatory democracy was remarkably similar to the rightist demand for decentralization.

But by 1966, the differences had become definitive. The New Left had become rigidly politicized, its dogma growing out of an eclectic blend of Trotskyism, anarchism, and romanticized teachings of Fidel, Mao, Ché, and Ho. Thus, common grounds and common sympathies were no longer possible. The New Left became increasingly terrorist and revolutionary, and as it did, the New Right, first coalescing behind Ronald Reagan in California in sufficient numbers to elect him governor, increasingly defined itself by reacting to the perceived threat posed by the New Left. This opposition, in turn, increasingly came to define American politics and dictated the terms of the national debate. On one side, so it seemed by the early seventies, were the New Leftists, their uneasy allies in the media and in the universities, and the new-breed politicians such as George McGovern, and on the other, the hard hats, the blue-collar types in general, the middle class, the old-line liberals and disillusioned Democrats, and the conservative Republicans. These forces clashed for the last time in 1972, and for a moment it seemed as if Nixon and Agnew had actually succeeded in fashioning a New American Majority out of the results. But then came Watergate, that majority broke once again into its disparate constituencies, and today what is left intact finds nourishment primarily in the Reagan wing of the Republican party, an articulate but tiny percentage of the American electorate. Nor has the New Left fared much better, its hard core today either underground or institutionalized into the McGovern wing of the Democratic party.

Nevertheless, during the decade in which it flourished, the New Left movement had a profound effect on our society. It was responsible, more than any other single factor, for ending our involvement in Vietnam. It drove one Democratic President into premature retirement and, ironically, insured the election of Richard Nixon, who could not have beaten Hubert Humphrey in 1968 without the demonstrations at the convention in Chicago that doomed Humphrey's campaign before it began.

Without the New Left, there would have been no outraged cry from Middle Americans for the restoration of order. Without the New Left, hundreds of thousands of traditional Democrats would not have crossed over to vote for the law and order Nixon-Agnew ticket. Without the New Left there would have been no Nixon-Agnew administration, no Haldeman-Ehrlichman-Mitchell-Dean, no Huston plan, no tapes, no Watergate. And without the New Left, it is very probable that there would be no Carter administration.

The New Left was responsible for Richard Nixon, who was elected primarily to put down what an increasingly large number of Americans had come to see as revolutionary excesses—excesses that, they believed, rightly or wrongly, represented a tangible threat to the structure of American society. And Richard Nixon responded by doing precisely what he was hired to do—he calmed the nation. His was essentially a counterrevolutionary administration, voted into office to carry out what by definition was a negative task. His job was to end things, to draw the line, to shout enough, and that is what he did. The other things that his supporters point to as accomplishments—the China initiative, for instance—may have been acts worthy of applause. But those were not the things he was elected to do, and in the end they were viewed as politically irrelevant. His job was to end the uprisings, to restore order, to cut back, to quiet down.

This he succeeded in doing, but in the end that wasn't enough. The riots and the demonstrations were over, undercut by the defusing of the war issue. But the hatred was still thick, still intense, and in the last act of his administration, Nixon seemed to draw all that hatred of a decade into himself and then pushed the self-destruct button. And now he sits Job-like on the ash heap in San Clemente. Today there's no longer a focal point for that hatred. Ironic, that he succeeded so well in a way that he would never have dreamed of. Or that most of us who worked for him could never have imagined possible.

But now its all over for many of us, Left and Right. It's an odd period for us all. There's a sense of disorientation, of dislocation, even a peculiar nostalgia for that Nixonian context, for things as they were, with those sharp, clear, hard convictions that once made us so sure of ourselves and the causes we embrace.

"The corruption and incompetence of our recent Presidencies is only a talisman of the wider loss of faith," writes Michael Rossman, a founder of the Free Speech Movement, "while people plod numbly on waiting for something, or clutch small fragments of reality of the incipient chaos."

For those of us on both sides, the adrenaline no longer flows. Richard Nixon's self-destruction cleared the air, Gerald Ford successfully mopped up, and the way was open for a new politician saying new things to establish what appears to be a government of national reconciliation. That politician was Jimmy Carter, and in his approach to social programs, he co-opted many of the most popular positions of the liberal Left. And in his appeal to values and morality and in his championing of human rights, he also took the conservative high ground.

What the Carter administration will finally do to the shape

of our government and the structure of our society remains anyone's guess. One suspects that we will get what we deserve and that it may be beneficial. But it is certain that his election signals the end of a decade, and that for many of us who once lived on adrenaline, things will never be the same again. Some of us have traveled a long way down a one-way street, and today the entrance has been sealed off. The Nixon-Agnew administration drew off the high emotionalism of a decade, and it already is extremely difficult to remember just what it felt like, living in that Nixonian context.

CHAPTER TWO

ODD, that those of us who began the decade so critical of our central government and the universities ended by being the fiercest defenders of those institutions. But perhaps that's inherent in conservatism. One conservative thinker, in fact, maintains that the ultimate role of conservatives in an essentially liberal society, as ours is, is to conserve liberalism.

Perhaps. But those of us who began as Democrats and ended as Nixon-Agnew supporters, as I did, were not conservatives—at least not in the currently accepted ideological definition of the term. William Buckley is a conservative, his positions based on faith, reason, and tradition. Those of us who formed that New American Majority, however, were something else entirely—reactionaries, if you will, or counterrevolutionaries. Faith, reason, tradition—all, no doubt, had something to do with making us what we were. But at the heart of it all was emotion.

The politics, the movements, the events of the past decade will be discussed and analyzed intensely for years to come, for the sixties and early seventies, beginning with Vietnam and the Free Speech Movement and ending with Watergate and the resignation of a President and a Vice-President, were watershed years in American history. There are many keys to that period. But in the last analysis, the single most important key may be emotion. Emotions *were* the period, and perhaps that's why it's so difficult to recapture the context within which the decade was played out. Emotions, like the political movements they give rise to, flare up quickly and are capable of searing the imagination. But they also fade rapidly, and once they are gone, it's extremely difficult to recapture the moments they illuminated.

The images from the past decade, already difficult to evoke, are images that once assaulted the emotions—street lights gleaming off the bayonets of national guard rifles stacked in the streets of Berkeley; a girl pushing a flower into a guardsman's rifle barrel; glass from smashed windows glittering along Telegraph Avenue; the screams and gunshots and bloodshed of People's Park; the almost sexual frenzy of the 5,000 students and street people packed into Sproul Plaza as Eldridge Cleaver whipped them up, something like contempt gleaming in his hard slitted eyes; the near-homicidal rages that swept through the SDS rallies when it began to appear that Nixon and Kissinger were beating them.

Perhaps this is why so many of the arguments of the sixties seem so esoteric and anachronistic today. It was a neoemotional, romantic decade, opening with the emotional rhetoric of a young activist President, proceeding through the high emotionalism and the romanticism of the civil rights and black power movements, exploding into emotional confrontations in Chicago, Oakland, Washington, and Kent State.

It was a decade of rage, of screams of tears. There were tears for John Kennedy. There were tears for Martin Luther King. There were tears for Robert Kennedy. There were tears for the children at Kent State. Seldom have our national emotions throbbed so continually close to the surface. There was the overt rage of the Weatherpeople, the growing rage implicit in the hard-hat counterdemonstrations, the rage channeled into the Wallace campaign in sufficient quantities to make him, by the end of the decade, the most formidible vote getter in the Democratic primaries. The emotions were raw and everywhere apparent, and as the decade progressed they turned increasingly hard. The sixties began with the love of the flower children and ended with a hatred that many still called love. Charles Manson and his girls, who swam easily in the radical social sea of the sixties, butchered their victims in the name of love, and Bernadine Dohrn applauded.

"The new sensibility has become a political factor," said Herbert Marcuse.

And indeed it had—and as much a political factor on the Right as on the Left. Reagan, Wallace, Agnew—all spoke to the emotions. And it was the new sensibility, as it became definitive on the Left, that pushed so many of us right. It had become a cliché on the liberal Left to say that the Right had created "an atmosphere of hate and fear" in which violence was inevitable. For over two decades, professors such as Richard Hofstadter and Daniel Bell—the latter now considered a conservative by his peers—routinely warned us against rightist paranoid politics and "violence cults on the Right," preparing us for assaults from rightist extremists. But then came the sixties and the violence, and as Dr. S. I. Hayakawa points out, our intellectual establishment, like the British at Singapore, discovered that their guns had been trained in the wrong direction.

"The American riots of the 1960's baffled political historians for lack of a clearly defined purpose," wrote Theodore White in 1968. "More parochially, American political scientists and historians found difficulty in framing the perspectives of the new American forms of mass violence because of the set of American history. For generations, violence had threatened America from the native American right—the menace always perceived on the lunatic fringe of reaction where Ku Klux Klan, American Nazis and Minutemen muttered, rumbled and mobilized as phantom marauders. But when the real marauders, in the 1960's, took to the streets, they came not from the 'right' but from the 'left' in the most liberal administration in history, while the thinkers looked the other way."

As White points out, the "set of American history," as established by the liberal academics, simply made no provision for the possibility of violence from the Left. To those of us with conservative tendencies, this had always seemed either an incredibly obtuse or incredibly dishonest mind set. Professor Hofstadter, for instance, spoke frequently during the sixties of "the commitment to nonviolence on the left." Yet surely, we thought, this was patently absurd. Hungary, Czechoslovakia, China, Cuba, Tibet, Russia—the history of the twentieth century, in fact, could be read in large part as the history of leftist violence. "Historically," wrote Hofstadter, "violence has not been an effective weapon of the Left." An oddly myopic statement indeed, for it seemed to many of us that in fact violence had been the *only* effective weapon of the Left.

This academic leftist tilt has never been quite satisfactorily explained. Perhaps it exists simply because liberalism, which is the fashionable academic ideology, is the popularized, watered-down, secular version of Marxism, the quintessential ideology of the Left. This is not to say that academics are—or were—to any significant degree committed Marxists. Most of them simply feel comfortable hewing to the fashionable pop-intellectual political line, just as back in the fifties they felt comfortable wearing tweed jackets and smoking pipes.

But, at any rate, today it may all be irrelevant. Jimmy Carter's hard line on human rights has had a salutary effect on liberal single-sightedness; today it has become fashionable to acknowledge that only iron-fisted repression holds the world's premier leftist system, the Soviet Union, together. True, there is still a romance with the equally repressive regime in China, but there has always been a romantic feeling toward oppressive regimes in the Third World. Some, of course, would say there is something slightly paternalistic or perhaps even racist in this romantic tolerance of Third World excesses, and others would maintain that the liberal blinkers cannot be said to have been removed until the day we come to grips with such phenomena as the rape of Tibet, one of the most barbarous events of the century.

Nevertheless, today there seems to be a new honesty, a new willingness to call repression by its name without finding excuses for it. And this not only affects the Left. It also puts pressure on the Right. Previously, as in the case of nations like Greece or Chile, for instance, in which rightist regimes have been no more repressive than regimes of the Left, the Right has been able to assail liberals for applying a double standard, the more lenient one being reserved for the regimes of the Left. In light of Carter's steady pressure on the Soviet Union, however, this argument has lost much of its impact, and today both Left and Right step much more gingerly when approaching the human rights issue.

In the sixties, however, while those who explain things to us continued to peer steadfastly rightward, the violence surged off the campuses and into the streets from the Left. There were, in those days, all manner of arguments advanced, primarily by the academics themselves, to explain precisely why that activity, which was raging across their campuses, frequently taking the form of beatings, firebombings, and riots, wasn't really violence at all. Professor Marcuse called it a natural reaction to something he named "repressive tolerance." Others, among them Berkeley's Professor Richard Lichtman, explained that campus and street violence was equivalent to what the university did to students and blacks and what the government was doing in Vietnam. Violence, in fact, could only be committed by institutions, not by individuals protesting institutionalized violence.

Perhaps. But at Berkeley in the sixties we lived with what looked very much like violence on a daily basis. Classes were disrupted as a matter of course, and it was not uncommon for those protesting such disruptions to be badly roughed up. Buildings were occupied, some were blown up, and bricks frequently sailed through library and classroom windows. As the decade drew on, the level of that violence increased, and it grew increasingly dangerous to walk the streets of Berkeley. It seemed to some of us very much like violence. And we knew precisely where that violence was coming from.

True, there was also counterviolence, but this occurred primarily to prevent vandalism and destruction, and its perpetrators were primarily poorly trained deputies. The Berkeley police force, manned by young college types, seldom bruised a student. And even in Chicago, where what has frequently been described as a "police riot" broke out, the "pigs," as they were called, reacted under extreme provocation from some of the most extreme and violent of the New Left groups. That does not excuse them, to be sure. But as Michael Lerner has pointed out, while those demonstrators in the streets were our children, so too were those "pigs."

The day-to-day violence with which we lived in the sixties at Berkeley naturally affected our daily lives, and for many it became the central fact of existence, coloring our views of everything around us, and, inevitably, our reactions were emotional. Some of us finally went shouting and crying into the streets to join what we viewed as the revolution, as was the case, finally, with the thousands of formerly uninvolved students who at the shooting of James Rector took to the streets to fight for the People's Park. Others of us, for similarly emotional reasons, moved in precisely the opposite direction.

I had been moving in that direction, I realize now, since first coming to Berkeley in 1966. But 1968 was the crucial year. There had been a devastating series of riots in the community, as the New Left moved off the campus and into the streets, preparing for the great confrontation that was to occur in Chicago later in the year. The antiwar movement at Berkeley had become unapologetically pro-Hanoi, actively rooting for North Vietnamese victories and refusing to discuss the consequences of such victories to the young Americans without college deferments who were fighting there. The civil rights movement had splintered into violent black racist groups that increasingly took pleasure in savaging whites on Bay-area campuses. The peace marches had become wild trashing raids, with the clenched fist replacing the peace sign. the SDS (Students for a Democratic Society) and other New Leftist groups had begun to arm, and those sweet songs of protest sung by Joan Baez and her imitators had given way to the Rolling Stones' "Street Fighting Man."

The summer of '68 in Berkeley was a summer of high emotions, and as I write this, two scenes from that summer come back vividly. In one of them I am sitting with a group of friends in the Heidelberg on Telegraph Avenue. The table is covered with empty Carlsberg bottles, and it is nearly closing time. We have been sitting there since noon, drinking and shouting. Bobby Kennedy, for whom I voted in the California primary, has been murdered. It is the day after the murder, and we are holding a wake.

Many of us felt something very special for Bobby, who in 1968 seemed to represent the last chance for building some sort of coalition capable of holding the country together. But his murder ended all that, and our wake for him was also a wake for something much larger that we felt had been permanently lost. And so we drank too much and became maudlin; the drinking allowed us to cry a bit for Bobby. A few days later, on its front page, a radical newspaper depicted him as a dead pig, and the tears gave way to what at the time seemed to be a permanent feeling of anger.

Another scene from that summer takes place during one of its periodic riots. A visiting professor, a very decent man, is talking to us about the causes of student unrest, his discussion coming from somewhere around 1959. But the juxtaposition of his civil observations, a decade out of date, with the screams and explosions from outside isn't quite real. It is almost as if we're characters in a Flaubert novel, each of us acting on a clearly defined level distinctly separate from the levels above and beneath it.

I leave the class and walk down Telegraph, past a group of street people who are shouting obscenities at a tense cop. The windows have been broken in most of the buildings, the sidewalks glitter with shattered glass, and the smell of tear gas is heavy in the air. A bunch of hard-looking kids walk up to me and demand some money. "Give us some change, man," they say. I refuse and they shout at my back.

I turn around, recross the campus, and walk toward our apartment in married student housing, about three miles away. For the first time, the trashers have moved well out of the campus-Telegraph area, ranging down University Avenue, smashing windows indiscriminately. One that had been smashed on this raid was the large plate glass window in the shop of a small, bent old man with an Eastern European accent who collected and sold violins. He was a gentle and trusting man, who liked to stand in his doorway and chat with passersby. Once, as I walked to campus, he handed me a stack of checks in stamped envelopes and asked me to mail them for him. He had never seen me before.

On this day, after the trashing expedition, he stood near his door, fondling a damaged violin, his eyes wet and bewildered.

It was the sum total of things like this that did it. Like the visiting professor, I realized that I was a decade out of date. I had come to Berkeley prepared to be sympathetic to many of the demands and goals of the Free Speech Movement. But after months of almost daily assaults on people and things that bore no relation to those demands and goals, I realized it was all up for me and people like me at Berkeley. My own beliefs were simple, perhaps naive. I believed that at some point patriotism had to be unquestioning. I believed our government and our political system to be the finest yet devised by man, and I believed absolutely that the men charged with running our government and our political system were sincere and totally dedicated men who, no matter what their personal idiosyncracies, could be trusted to do their very best for their country.

It was a good country, a good society. Certainly, we had problems. But we were still the best-fed, best-clothed, best-housed, best-educated nation on earth, a nation in which anyone could still rise, as Agnew liked to say, as high as his abilities and talents could take him. ("To our parents," said Agnew in a speech I had written for delivery to a New York ethnic group, "America was the land of opportunity, the land in which, unlike many of the countries they had left, a man could rise just as high as his abilities and determination carried him. As a boy during the depression I remember watching my father return late each evening after a long day's work, dead tired but never discouraged, determined to make the best possible life for his family in his adopted country. And he succeeded, succeeded so well that I am able to stand here tonight as Vice-President of the United States.")

The words and the concepts they denote seem inadequate as I write them now. But when in that summer of '68 in

Berkeley I found myself forced by what went on around me to return to first principles, there it was, as simple as that. The reaction, of course, was an emotional one, prompted by daily events. Yet that reaction seemed then—and seems today—at least as valid as the reactions that sent the New Left into the streets, for in the end both reactions sprang from the individual, the personal.

The New Leftists took to the streets to rid the world of racism, repression, poverty. Yet that racism, repression, and poverty had nothing to do with their own lives. They were, for the most part, well-off, white, middle-class children, who had been accustomed to receiving as a matter of course the good things of life from their parents. As one commentator noted at the time, this was the first revolution in the history of the world in which the revolutionaries drove to the barricades in Mustangs. They knew little of poverty and nothing of repression, and their notions of racism were hopelessly naive, tied up with a vision of the black man as romantic and as far removed from reality as James Fenimore Cooper's picture of the red man. They were, as Tom Wolfe points out, the freest generation the world has seen, their activities possible nowhere else on earth.

And perhaps, in the end, that explains a great deal about it. Perhaps they were just too free, and it was that freedom, expanding with every generation since the forties, which finally proved too much to handle. It may be, in fact, that it was that freedom against which the New Left was rebelling. Perhaps the New Left revolution was more than anything else a revolt against liberalism. Trendy views of childrearing had helped shape their early lives. In their schools the emphasis was increasingly on creativity and less on traditional modes of learning. And on the university campuses, although administrators did their best to lock students into their computers, freedom was almost total, and thus, in an odd way, the college experience became increasingly impersonal.

Perhaps more than anything else it was the desire for personalization, the desire to live a full individual life framed by standards and principles, the sort of life rendered increasingly difficult by relativistic teachings and an encroaching liberal administrative technocracy, that helped fuel the revolt of the sixties. And perhaps this is why the New Leftists, most of whom were comfortable middle-class children whose direct experience of life was minimal, were enamored of repressive, neo-Marxian collectivist models. They took to the streets in the name of freedom. But the sorts of regimes they championed and apparently dreamed of living under were among the most authoritarian, repressive, and inhumane the world has seen. And as the romantic spawn of the middle class, they would have been first to go under such regimes.

But no matter. Whole textbooks could be written on the motivations and the drives of both sides. What is important to remember is that in those days the threat seemed very real. The New Left believed a revolution of sorts was on, and so did most Americans, who watched the revolution unfold on nightly television news installments. And it all seemed especially real to those of us who had to walk through the revolution each day as we attempted, with a growing feeling of futility, to find some relation between the things we studied and the things that were going on around us. And for those of us with children, it was extremely difficult, for with every riot, every trashing, we grew increasingly fearful for our children's future and for the future of the society into which we would soon send them.

Whether the country embodied all those evils against which the New Left inveighed remains a moot question. But for those of us on the other side, their view of our society seemed exclusively focused on a few rotten spots that could neatly be cut out, and were, in fact, being cut out even as the troops took to the street. Relations between the races had been steadily improving; Americans were showered with an array of federally subsidized benefits undreamed of two decades earlier; the law had expanded to protect rights that no other society on earth had ever dreamed of calling rights.

Those of us who had come from working families, who were veterans, who were raising families, who had worked at a variety of jobs, who had seen something of the world beyond the university campus—we knew that things were getting better, just because our own lives were getting better.

And we also knew that there were social ills much closer at hand than the more abstract ills against which the New Left inveighed. We knew that there was something basically wrong when we were prevented from receiving the education we had paid for because one group of people decided to close our universities down. We knew there was something wrong in indiscriminate trashing which left gentle old men in tears. We knew there was something wrong in preaching violence and terrorism, which invariably led to destruction and assassination. The New Left accused the "establishment" of perpetrating violence. But the incivility, the inhumanity, and the violence we encountered on the campuses on a daily basis were invariably perpetrated by the New Left.

Toward the end of the sixties, and into the seventies, when we could take no more, many of us finally rebelled. Some, no longer able to stomach it all, voted for George Wallace. (Ironically enough, most of the people were blue-collar workers, the closest thing there is in America to a proletariat.) Others among us, although registered Democrats, voted for Nixon-Agnew, the idea being that unlike Wallace, Nixon might put down the revolution without bringing on a real—as opposed to the imagined—repression.

In 1968, I voted for Nixon-Agnew, my first straight Republican vote. No doubt it sounds overdone to say so, but at the time I believed I was also casting that vote for Bobby Kennedy. And it was also in that year, after the series of riots that led to the trashing of the violin shop, that I began to submit articles to *National Review*. I didn't know then, of course, that those articles would result in a job at *National Review*, which would in turn lead to jobs in Washington with Agnew, Nixon, and Ford. At the time, I wrote them for therapeutic reasons, unable, any longer, to walk the Berkeley campus talking to myself. There were two sides to the campus story, but only one was being told, and it seemed extremely important—even, in those days, essential—to get the viewpoint of the other side on paper.

CHAPTER THREE

THE Nixon-Agnew experience was an emotional roller coaster. But toward the end of that period other things had intruded, and the emotions were neither sharp nor clear, and frequently dishonest. It wasn't Berkeley.

Strange, to feel nostalgia for a place and a period and a state of mind that epitomized everything that seemed most loathsome during the past decade. But perhaps anything experienced purely leaves a permanent mark, and after that experience much of life consists of trying to duplicate it—not the experience itself, of course, but the feeling that accompanied it. And perhaps that's why, since I left a decade ago, I've returned to Berkeley at least once a year—perhaps I left something there ten years ago, and if I could find it again, much of what has happened over the last few years would make sense.

But it's not possible, of course. It's all over at Berkeley. The context is missing, surviving these days only at San Clemente and a few isolated centers.

It's not that Berkely has been deradicalized. It still is and always will be the radical capital of America. But that intensity, that concentrated hatred of a decade ago, has blown away. Berkeley is as funky and offbeat as ever. The strays still drift along Telegraph, panhandling change, and every now and then a deep-bush hippie troupe, living communally somewhere up north, will wander in to set up camp for a few days on the edge of campus and smoke their dope and sing. Pushers still peddle their goods in doorways, although the use of hard drugs is down sharply now. Oakland blacks still follow teen-age blondes down Telegraph, and the street is littered with vendors selling handmade jewelry, paintings, leather bags, hot pretzels, health foods, and fresh orange juice. The street bands are still there, every now and then a motorcycle gang roars through, and occasionally a purse gets snatched. But no one's angry.

On the campus, where once the New Left packed Sproul Plaza to do battle with the CIA, the Pentagon, the military-industrial complex, and the government in Washington, aging activist holdovers now hand out pamplets protesting the construction—not of a nuclear plant—but of a MacDonald's near campus. But the students just don't seem to care.

During my last visit, there was a disturbance, but it involved a beer fight between fraternity and sorority types, who during the sixties kept a very low profile. During the same week, campus guards found a couple—heterosexual—making love in the men's room of Wheeler Hall. And a man was taken into custody for peeping up women's skirts in Moffit Library.

The brightest leftist group on campus these days is the Trotskyist Spartacist Youth League. One of its members tells me that the students have become apolitical, and as a result the administration has begun to institute repressive measures, such as limiting the size of fund-raising tables on Sproul Plaza. And what remains of the old New Left is hopelessly splintered into small, feuding ineffectual groups, some of them caught up in personality cultism, others into "hippie life-stylism." Few students bother any longer to stop for the Sproul Plaza noontime rallies that once attracted thousands. The issues just aren't there. There is no war, the women's movement has crested, no one cares about Cesar Chavez or grapes any longer, blacks aren't big this year, and there's an administration in Washington that's backing the Left into a corner on the human rights issue. (The Spartacists, desperate, try to convince us the "the deformed workers' states" of the East are still superior to what we have. But the Solzhenitsyns and the Bukovskys make it difficult. Berkeley just isn't Gulag, no matter how you cut it.)

The ideological fervor has evaporated. The *Berkeley Barb*, once the nation's single most important organ of the New Left, now devotes a third of an issue to ads for massage parlors and kinky sex. Startling. And even more startling is what has replaced it. Today the best publication in Berkeley is *Radix*, a monthly put out by the Berkeley Christian Coalition, many of the members of which are converts who once served in the old New Left.

Back in the sixties, the only consistently visible spokesman for militant Christianity on campus was Brother Hubert, a sunburned, gap-toothed gentleman who attempted daily to trumpet the good news over the shouts and jeers of thousands of militants. Today, however, one of the busiest places on Telegraph is Logos, a Christian bookstore. True, there is a decided leftward tilt to the social gospel as preached at Berkeley. But at Berkeley, Jacob Javits is a right-winger, and the wonder is that this thriving Christian movement exists at all. It is, perhaps, part of the peculiar new context that Carter is helping to synthesize.

I like it very much, and I regret in many ways that I've gone too far down that one-way road to fit comfortably within it. But I wouldn't mind seeing my children there at all.

Changes. And perhaps the most noticeable change of all is how different the students look. During the sixties everyone looked fourty-five years old. But now they look like kids again. That look, of course, is still distinctly northern California, one of the most distinctive looks in the United States. But it's a bit cleaner, just a bit straighter, and not at all frazzled. Perhaps, above all, it's the faces—they're *happy* faces, and the kids seem to enjoy wearing them. During the sixties, a happy face would have been grounds for expulsion from the Young Socialists Alliance.

It occurs to me, as I watch the students, that many of them would have been seven or eight years old during the great days of the New Left uprisings. I feel a pang, and recall an anecdote. At the time of the Frost-Nixon interviews, my son was walking along a road near our home in Maryland. A battered old bus plastered with faded peace stickers passed him slowly, and the driver and his passenger leaned out and gave him the peace sign. What struck him most, he told us later, was their hair—it was long and totally gray. They were old men. He had, he was convinced, just seen the last of the hippies.

On the Berkeley campus, in 1977, I felt very much like the last of the reactionaries.

A final scene from that last visit to Berkeley, one which brought the last days of Richard Nixon very much to mind.

I had walked around campus, revisiting the scenes of the confrontations of the sixties, and had paused before a small unobtrusive building sandwiched in among several larger ones. The building was Moses Hall, and in 1968, it briefly became the center of national media attention when it was occupied by New Leftists, protesting a Regents' decision to prohibit Eldrige Cleaver from teaching a course on racism on campus for credit.

The Moses Hall confrontation was the first I had watched as a reporter rather than as just a spectator, and the scenes from the night, just before Halloween, were still vivid.

It had been a nervous week on campus. Traveling New Leftists like Mark Rudd had visited campus to whip up emotions, miniriots exploded along Telegraph, most classes had been disrupted, and there were a number of fitful sit-ins.

On October 23, the atmosphere was electric, no one went to classes, and thousands of demonstrators and curious students, street people, and sightseers milled around the campus. Suddenly, for no single reason, a great roar went up and thousands of people began to race across campus, closing several buildings as they ran. After a number of unsuccessful attempts to occupy buildings, several hundred of the more militant types took Moses Hall. They stood in the two irregular turrets, waving Vietcong banners and black flags of anarchy, which were supplied, so the story went, by members of the TV crews, who were busy filming the scene.

As it grew dark, screaming students and street people ripped up fences and scaffolding and anything that would burn and built bonfires, around which they began to dance and chant, the chants alternating between obscenities and strange animal ululations.

By ten o'clock there were thousands of people ringing Moses Hall, professors and sightseers and newsmen mingling with students and demonstrators and street people, who grew increasingly frenzied as the night wore on, sucking on pot, dancing around their bonfires, and throwing rocks and bricks at any available window. As the scene grew progressively wilder, it became impossible to tell the spectators from the participants. Figures wove in and out of the flickering paths of light cast by TV lights and bonfires, and just out of the light, in shadowy patches of grass, dozens of couples began to copulate. It was eerie, mindless, nauseating, as if one had suddenly been transported back in time to an ancient Celtic heath upon which the witches and warlocks and deformed and demented creatures from the forest capered obscenely in the moonlight. And it may have been this atavism, which so frequently accompanied New Left actions, that ended by forcing so many of us to take a stand.

Today, Moses Hall is just Moses Hall, but as I walk by, the scenes return vividly, and suddenly there are other scenes from August 1974, which at first seem to arouse some of the same emotions. But this time there was no context.

It is my last day as a Nixon speechwriter, the last day of a wild and irrational year. Ray Price is in his office at the other end of the old Executive Office Building, putting the final touches on the resignation speech. Most of us spend the day wandering from office to office, drinking and telling bitter jokes. We joke about martial law, about asking Brezhnev for a first strike, about arresting the White House press corps for treason.

The speechwriters also joke about not having to go through with the final project. There was always, up to the end, a project that would help turn the tide. This one we did not relish, but it had been forced on us by what we perceived to be the total incompetence of Nixon's lawyers.

During the last months the EOB had been filling up with imported legal help, until they finally occupied one whole corridor and had converted a large suite into a full-fledged law library. Yet even the best of them seemed decidedly second rate. St. Clair, for instance, despite his reputation, had attempted until nearly the end to defend his client without listening to the tapes—which meant, of course, that he was in no position at all to help the client for whom he was arguing. And most of the rest were decidedly third-rate, roaming the halls like tourists, eager to get back home and tell what they'd seen.

One of them, a young, obscure lawyer from Texas, has told every newsman in sight that he would single-handedly save the President, and arrived at the EOB eager to show us all his press clippings. He dropped by my office one day to tell me that he was about to give an in-depth interview to someone named John Osborne, who couldn't help but be sympathetic, since he wrote for a magazine called *The New Republican.*

His courtroom heroics never came to pass, however. He spends several weeks grumbling about the slowness of his paychecks, breaks his foot on a radiator in his hotel room while running in place, and soon thereafter limps slowly back to the Southwest.

Most of the others stick around, however, despite frequent staff attempts to hurry their departure. Ben Stein, a speechwriter and a lawyer himself, who has worked on Nixon's taxes, was appalled at the ineptitude of two of the imported lawyers with whom he had been asked to work. Ben calls Julie, explains that these lawyers are doing her father a disservice, and asks her to pass it on.

Later, the two lawyers visit Ben to thank him profusely for putting in a good word for them. They had had a call from the President, praising them for their good work. Ben, stunned, asked Julie what happened. Daddy just got it all mixed up, she explains.

The lawyers simply weren't up to the job, although it wasn't all their fault, for it was extremely difficult to determine just what the job was. As the staff saw it, however, the job was to try to do whatever could be done to prevent the President from being run out of town on a rail. And so someone talked us into taking on the final project, part of which we believed should have been handled by the lawyers—although, as it turned out, it didn't make the slightest difference at all who handled it.

The idea was that half the writing staff—Dave Gergen, Noel Koch, and Ben Stein—would sift through the stacks of material compiled during the House impeachment hearings, pinpointing the legal weaknesses, and then Ken Khachigian, Aram Bakshian, and I would write speeches highlighting those weaknesses and pointing out that if a President were to be impeached on the basis of such flawed evidence, the Republic would surely collapse. The speeches, scores of them, would be written for any sympathetic representatives or senators willing to read them.

It was not an appealing project. For one thing, the stacks of material to be sifted through were as tall as several basketball players. For another, we could count the senators and representatives willing to read those scores of speeches, each of course written in the appropriate regional idiom, on the fingers of one hand. It's not that they thought such practices unethical. A significant portion of speeches given on the floor of the House and Senate are—or at lease were—written by White House speechwriters. A few days before, I had written what was the last such speech in defense of Nixon, to be read by Senator Scott of Virginia. Scott, the last legislator to request a pro-Nixon speech, had been voted, no doubt unfairly, the dumbest man in the Senate. And he may also have been Nixon's last defender on the Hill.

The last day wears on. We wander from office to office, drinking, watching the blanket coverage on television, the newsmen strangely subdued and jittery, as if the enormity of what they have helped bring on suddenly has hit them. There is little or no crowing—not even from Dan Rather, whose loathing for Nixon, which was returned in spades, made those presidential press conferences crackle. Rather, in fact, seems strangely subdued, perhaps sensing that his career, along with Nixon's, might be over. That career had consisted, toward the end, of covering Nixon, and the coverage was so intensely personal, so emotional, that it was difficult to see where Rather would fit in it all once Nixon had gone—or, for that matter, who would want him fitting in it. And in the end, one suspects, that that is why CBS has relegated him to a low-profile in New York. Rather, who, like Roger Mudd, once aspired to Cronkite's job, has suffered the fate of all those, friend or foe, who became caught up in that emotional context.

During the last day, the crowds gather again on Pennsylvania Avenue. Since the smoking-gun tape, there has been something like a vigil outside the White House compound—hundreds of people gathering daily to press up against the fences and stare at the buildings. Sometimes we watch them watching us out the window. Sometimes we watch TV to watch them watching us.

It is nearly time for the speech. Most of the secretaries are crying. It has been a week for crying. Tonight the President's family is crying in the White House. Earlier, General Haig had called us all together in the EOB conference room to tell us about the "smoking-gun tape" and to thank us for carrying on. His voice was unsteady and there were tears in his eyes. It was touching, no doubt about it. But in retrospect, Haig, telling us how proud he was of us for having done our duty, is somehow like Smiling Jack saying farewell to a squadron of fighter pilots.

The EOB has filled up with wandering people. Ben Stein, not a drinker, walks by carrying an open bottle of scotch. It's the first time we can remember seeing a Nixon staffer walking through the White House compound with an open bottle.

Some of the husbands and wives of staffers have begun to arrive. My wife and I visit several offices and have a number of drinks; then we go to Dave Gergen's office to watch the speech on television. Bill Safire and Ben Stein come in to watch, and we all have something to drink. When Nixon has finished, we agree it was a good and dignified speech and that the press reaction to it seemed uncharacteristically low-key.

Ben doesn't agree. "My God," he moans, sprawling on the couch as a TV commentator makes a banal remark. "Have they no mercy?" Ben genuinely liked Nixon, and the next morning he cried as Nixon said his final, peculiar farewell to his staff, putting on his glasses in public for the first time, quoting "Old T.R.," and lingering on images of death. (The writing department was once asked to compile a list of Nixon's hundred favorite anecdotes. A good half of them concerned adversity and death.) During the first days under Ford, Ben, before he quit to go to the *Wall Street Journal*, would ask the White House corps detachment to play the tape of that farewell over and over. Since these replays always came over one of the open TV channels, the new Ford staffers found themselves frequently switching on the rerun of Nixon's farewell, something that made them very nervous. On his last day in the EOB, Ben spent the morning in his office, running the farewell over and over, and crying.

Later, after the speech, Ken Khachigian and his wife and Pat and I go out for drinks and food. We decide on Trader Vic's, for a number of reasons. It was the only restaurant in Washington that Richard Nixon liked—and that, of course, gave the tastemakers fits. Reagan liked it, Agnew liked it. It is quintessentially Californian, and it is quintessentially Republican. California is the state in which the new conservative movement first solidified, and during the '64 convention, the Goldwater brain trust plotted the capture of the Republican party at Trader Vic's in San Francisco. And as a result of their success, Richard Nixon was the nominee in 1968.

Trader Vic's also means a great deal to me—one of those places, like O'Hare Airport, where I always seem to find myself during important periods of personal change.

After several of my Berkeley pieces had appeared in *National Review*, William Buckley came to San Francisco, we met at Trader Vic's there, and after we drank several glasses of navy grog, he asked me to come to work at his magazine. Several years later, over navy grogs at Trader Vic's in Washington, Spiro Agnew asked me to join his staff. Thus, it seemed appropriate to round it all off, to end it all in the way it had begun. And so we decide on Trader Vic's.

Outside, the streets are jammed with celebrants. "He *gone*, he *gone*," shouts one prancing black man. Pennsylvania Avenue has been cordonned off, and people are chanting, dancing, embracing. Girls ride on men's shoulders, and groups dance around bonfires burning on the sidewalks. And for a moment, it was 1968 again. There were those bonfires, those ululating cries, the shrieks. It was as if they'd all emerged from those basements and attics in which they'd all been hiding since the repression came down, chanting and capering once more. Then it was Moses Hall. Tonight it was the White House.

I push a path for us, shoving and snarling, and we come face to face with the prancing black man. "He *gone*, he *gone*," he shouts, waving his finger at us. "Boy," I shout back, "you no *good*." I begin to yell something incoherent at him that seems funny at the time, as my wife tries to tug me through the crowd. Suddenly, as I listen to myself shouting, I remember a scene from the night on which Moses Hall was occupied. I was standing next to a fat young man wearing a dress-blue marine corps jacket, little, round, green eyeglasses, and a maroon beret. He had been muttering incoherently, the volume increasing as the scene grew wilder. Suddenly, unable to contain it all, he began to jump straight up and down, screaming. Another lunatic, I thought then, and in many ways typical of the whole crowd. But now I find myself doing much the same thing. I don't have the jacket or the eyeglasses or the maroon beret. But I am screaming. It has, indeed, all come full circle.

Later, on the way back to the EOB, we stand behind a rope for a while and watch the celebrants along Pennsylvania and wonder if Nixon is looking out at them from some darkened White House window. If he is, we know there'll be no ambivalent feelings. These are still the demonstrators, the elitists, the SDSers, the rotten apples, the spawn of permissiveness, dancing around their bonfires, rooting for Hanoi, hoping to bring the Republic down. In the view from the White House, that old sixties context is still there, and the enemy is waiting to occupy the White House, just as they occupied Moses Hall. From the White House, they still look like *them*, but in the last days, everyone who isn't with us is one of them. No doubt that was precisely the way the SDSers felt during their last days.

From the street, however, the view is different. We have become the occupiers, and these people on Pennsylvania are waiting, as I once waited at Berkeley, for the officials to clear the occupiers out. There is now only one overriding threat to domestic tranquility, and that threat is no longer mounted by the former occupiers of Moses Hall.

Two girls standing near us beside the rope make some jokes about Nixon, and I snarl. But my wife tells them who I work for, and they say they understand and look at me with something very like pity. And that makes everything infinitely worse.

The next day, however, it was all gone, and I realized how terribly thin it had become during that last year. I slept on the morning of the departure and stayed in bed to watch Nixon's final farewell to us on TV. There was a close-up of Ben Stein crying.

I went into Washington around noon. There was an unpredicted shower that day, and for a while it poured, flooding the streets. Nixon had flashed the V for victory sign one last time and was somewhere en route to Casa Pacifica. Ford was in the process of taking over, and sure enough, there was that damned downpour, giving the feature writers their hook into the inevitable stories about the new, cleansing spirit. And in the White House compound, the Nixon pictures were coming down. It was 1974, ten years after the birth of the Free Speech Movement, and the sixties had finally ended.

That, in the last analysis, was the most significant accomplishment of the Nixon administration. And it was no small accomplishment, for it was precisely what the Administration was hired to do.

However, the problem was that the Administration had already done most of what it had to do toward the end of the first term, and in 1972 there were only two major items of domestic business left on the agenda. One was to prevent the worse of the aberrations of the sixties from becoming institutionalized into broad-based political movements, and this was largely accomplished by the destruction of McGovernism in the election of 1972. The other major piece of business was to clear the air, to dispel the lingering hatreds, and this was accomplished two years later, with the resignation.

The strength of the Nixon administration was also its weakness, making something like Watergate inevitable. It was a negative Administration, and it was not in business to develop what we like to call positive programs and policies. Richard Nixon was not elected to give people things, to construct new programs, to build new structures. He was hired to take away, to cut back, to restore order.

Rightly or wrongly, Americans believed they were caught up in a revolution and that their institutions were in danger of collapsing. That is difficult to believe today, for the revolutionary context has evaporated, a comfortable cloud of time has already blurred the excesses of the past decade, and we can no longer quite clearly recall the riots, the mobs in the streets, the President who could no longer venture into public, the assassinations, the tears.

But it was very real then, and many Americans believed their country was increasingly governed from the streets. It may not have been a revolution according to formal definition. But formal definitions of social phenomena tend to be anachronistic once they are generally accepted, and it seemed to the American majority that the seeds of a revolutionary situation had been planted and that it was time to destroy those seeds before they took root.

Thus Americans elected a counterrevolutionary government, and it was in this, putting down the perceived revolution—the primary task he was elected to perform—that Richard Nixon was successful. When he took office, the nation was exploding. When he left, the emotions had been drained, and it was suddenly very quiet.

In other areas, he was less successful. He had also been elected by the more hard-core among his backers to cut back on spending, to cut out wasteful programs, to trim the size of government, to reduce taxes, and to balance the budget. In the end, he did none of these things, and his attempt to play Disraeli cost him dearly among those who could have been expected to form the bedrock of his natural constituency.

His efforts during the last two years to out-Democrat the Democrats won him no new friends, and lost him many traditional allies. Nor did those great foreign policy initiatives provide him with a permanent new constituency, although, again, they did fracture the old one. The people who sent Nixon to Washington to restore order didn't care about and frequently disapproved of detente and SALT and openings to China. True, many of the achievements—and particulary the dash with which they were brought off—were applauded. Virtuoso performances are always applauded. But many of those applauding loudest were Nixon's natural enemies, and they remained enemies to the end, while those with the deepest reservations about those performances were Nixon's natural constituents, many of whom became permanently alienated.

Thus, during the last year in office, Nixon was a man who had lost his natural constituency and had failed to win a new one, and when the crunch came, the ardent supporters were few and far between. This is, of course, not entirely his fault. He was elected to carry out a negative chore, and once that chore had been carried out, there was no real reason for him to remain on the scene. But he could not, of course, just step down. Thus it was necessary to devise new reasons for keeping him in office, reasons entirely different from those that put him there in the first place.

This, essentially, is the problem faced by all governments put into office for counterrevolutionary purposes. Such governments have negative functions to carry out, the formulation of programs and policies is secondary, and the people who support such governments do so for emotional rather than programmatic reasons. Those of us who came to work for Agnew didn't do so because he had been a successful county executive or governor, or because he had a finely honed appreciation of intergovernmental relations, or because he had mastered the intricacies of revenue sharing. We came to him because he was the tribune of Middle America, come to put down insurrection and restore order.

But the problem for the counterrevoluntionary is that once he has restored order, there is nothing left for him to do. The people who asked him to do the job are sometimes satisfied, sometimes grateful, sometimes indifferent. But the unrest has been put down, and there is no longer an emotional context, without which the counterrevolutionary seems singularly out of place. This may present no problem in a certain sort of society, in which the hero of the moment rides off once the job is done. But in most societies, once the war is over, counterrevolutionary regimes tend to take several predictable courses. Some try to build what appears to be positive programs and policies on the foundation laid down by what is by definition a negative philosophy. This can be done, if you are a sufficiently skilled showman and have no Watergates to undercut you. But in the end you run the risk of appearing to have no center. People suspect that what you do has little to do with what you say, and you seem at best inconsistent and at worst devious. And when this happens, several things usually follow—you lose your base of power and reluctantly relinquish that power; you scramble to consolidate power by any means available, and in the process you precipitate a crisis that blows you away with little trace; or you blow yourself away.

Each of these things, in various ways, happened to Richard Nixon. When his job was done, the thrust of his administration became to consolidate power. But it was power for its own sake, power without relation to function, and in the end it brought on Watergate. That it happened was regrettable for the nation and tragic for Nixon. But given the job he was hired to do, given the nature of the regime required to do that job, given the structure of American politics and government, the outcome was perhaps inevitable. Nixon's counterrevolutionary presidency was good and necessary for the country. And so was his resignation.

And this, in the end, was Nixon's legacy. He wanted desperately, of course, for that legacy to be "the lasting structure of peace," which phrase he had us write into nearly every public statement. But that foreign policy of which he was so proud proved in the end to be in large part a juggling act, tied too closely to the political fortunes of one man. Ford, despite the intensive coaching of Henry Kissinger, could never quite learn the lines, couldn't keep the balls in the air. Without the leading actor the act fell flat, and today his Democratic successors scramble to put distance between themselves and the Nixon-Kissinger policies.

Nevertheless, although Nixon's legacy was a negative one, we have all derived positive benefits from it. He did not build a structure, he demolished one. In the process he destroyed himself, and by so doing, he cleared away the hatreds and tensions that had been building toward an explosion for a decade.

An era in American politics has come full circle, and it is not likely that we will soon again see a Moses Hall or a Chicago or a presidential resignation. That emotional context within which we functioned for more than a decade no longer rigidly shapes our daily lives. The emotions are still there, in abundance, and emotions, more than anything else, decided the outcome of the 1976 presidential election.

But they are no longer the intensely concentrated and negative emotions of the last decade. They have been diffused and softened by Nixon's catharsis; today they seem the more wistful and nostalgic emotions of a people yearning for a new beginning that incorporates the standards and values of our recent past, just before the ultraromantic surge of the past decade swept us off course.

The sixties are finally over, laid to rest by Watergate and the election of 1976, and today we are searching for a new context.

CHAPTER FOUR

EMOTIONS ran high during the final days, as each week brought a new round of mortar shells into the White House compound, and we lived on adrenaline, counterattacking an increasingly expanding field of attackers. But the context was very different. It was no longer a matter of real or imaginary revolutionary threats. The context now was the survival of one man, and few of us, no matter how rabid, could quite believe Dan Rather was a Weatherman.

The emotions were there, in abundance, flashing through our offices like heat lightning in July. But they had become shrill and febrile, feeding on themselves, emotions for their own sake with no real context. And like many of those who had seen themselves as members of the New Majority, my emotional supply was running low, having been drained in October 1973, by the disgrace and resignation of our spokesman, Spiro Agnew. His fall had stunned all of us who saw him as the last honest man in American politics, and as illogical as it may have been, our whole cause seemed suddenly suspect and soiled. We felt let down. But more than that, many of us felt ashamed. And shame may be the most enervating emotion of them all.

It ended for me on October 10, 1973, in a conference room in the old Executive Office Building, where General Mike

Dunn, Agnew's military aide, had called the Agnew staff together.

"Our leader is today resigning his high office," said Dunn. "He has asked me to thank you all."

There was a brief silence. Then David Keene, Agnew's political adviser, slapped the table loudly with his hand. "Don't you think he owes it to us to thank us himself?" he snapped. Several of the girls began to cry. And that was that.

Later that evening, I went out for a drink with Aram Bakshian, a Nixon speechwriter, and Suzy Cox, the only other surviving Agnew speechwriter. Perhaps it's a variation on the pathetic fallacy to say that a city has feelings. But Washington is a one-industry town, and when something significant happens within that industry, the message quickly flashes through the city's nervous system. Nothing in years had happened to equal Agnew's unprecedented resignation, and the city was quivering. The sidewalks were crowded, unusual for a weekday night in autumn, people seemed to be talking more loudly and laughing more than usual, and buildings that would normally have been dark were blazing with light.

We first went to the National Press Club, usually empty on Thursdays. But it had to be congressional night, and both bars were crowded with reporters and political types, drinking and laughing and shouting. And the word they shouted most frequently was "Agnew."

It was, obviously, no place for us that night, and we headed instead for the cocktail lounge at Nick and Dottie's, next to the Sans Souci on Seventeenth. But a friend of Suzy's, a young reporter from a Pennsylvania paper looking for feature material, insisted on tagging along. "How do you *feel*?" he kept asking. "Will you get the hell *out* of here," I shouted. He apologized profusely, but stayed with us. Ah, what the hell, I thought, and we all went to drink it off.

I had last seen Agnew toward the end of September. There were only a few days to go to his appearance before the Federation of Republican Women, and Suzy and I hadn't been able to come up with a speech. Each day brought a new wave of leaks, and increasingly there were rumors of an indictment, and rumors about plea bargaining. But we didn't want to believe that the Agnew we knew could by definition engage in plea bargaining. If he did, then he just wasn't Agnew. Nevertheless, it was a chaotic period, and we found we had nothing to say. And so three days before the speech he called us in to try to tell us what he'd like to say in Los Angeles.

He wanted to discuss our system of justice, he told us, and how its principles should apply equally to all men. But he also wanted to talk about the grand jury system, and how it could not function without secrecy. He wanted to talk about leaks. And he wanted to distinguish between indictment and guilt. "Most people," he said, "don't understand that indictment does *not* equal conviction."

He talked about a few more points that he wanted woven into his speech, and then began to talk about his situation. He mentioned a story that had appeared in that day's *Star-News*, which alleged that he had taken money from someone named Joel Kline. "I don't even *know* Joel Kline," he said. "In fact, I wouldn't know this Joel Kline if I *fell* over him."

He talked about the charges in general, complaining, as he frequently did, about lacking the money he required to live up to the demands of his position. "Do they think I keep it in coffee cans in my back yard?" he asked. "I wish I did. I'd go out and dig some of it up."

He talked about some of the evidence the investigation was turning up, including a list of neckties he'd bought. Then he began to talk about his mother-in-law. It was very hard, he told us with a forced grin, to come home each evening and sit down to dinner with his wife and her mother, knowing she had seen the stories in the papers. Then he began to talk about the time he had taken his mother-in-law along on a trip to Hawaii. The accommodations were luxurious, and he described them lovingly and in detail. (Later, Suzy remarked that only someone unused to luxury could remember and appreciate that sort of detail.) His mother-in-law, he told us, took it all in and then said: "I hope the taxpayers aren't paying for all this."

Then he put back his head and laughed. We all joined in, of

course. You always laugh when the Vice-President of the United States makes a joke. But it went on and on, and our laughs became strained and sputtered out, and for a minute he laughed alone. It was, said Suzy later, very much like a cry of anguish.

The small talk was finally exhausted, but he seemed reluctant to let us leave, almost as if he wanted to be absolutely certain that he still was to us what we had believed him to be.

As we stood up, he mentioned the speech again. "Remember, I want to be subtle. Keep it on a high plane." As we filed out, he said, "Play me some organ music, John."

Those were the last words I heard him say as Vice-President. He went to Los Angeles, played the organ music, then put down his text and gave a second speech, the famous "I will not resign if indicted" speech that brought his audience screaming to its feet. Fitting, I thought later, that on that penultimate public appearance, two Agnews appeared on that podium in Los Angeles at the same time.

"Play me some organ music." The association that ended with those words had begun in 1970. My first book, *The Kumquat Statement,* had just been published by Cowles. (Like the politicians I was later to work for, my publisher went bankrupt shortly after our association began.) Late in November, out of the blue, I had a phone call at my office at *National Review.* It was Spiro Agnew. He had just read *The Kumquat Statement.* He discussed the book with me for twenty minutes, laughed over some of the parts he found particularly funny, and told me that he was buying several hundred copies to give as Christmas presents.

I was stunned. He was, after all, the Vice-President of the United States, and Vice-Presidents don't call every day of the week. And he was also, at the moment, one of the most powerful and admired political figures in the country.

In his book *Cruising Speed,* Bill Buckley described it this way. "John Coyne is our California kid-watcher. He is very pleased this morning because a half hour ago he got a phone call from Spiro Agnew who told him that he, Agnew, had read *The Kumquat Statement*—Coyne's account of what happened at Berkeley, and what has happened generally at the hands of the kids—and thinks it splendid, which greatly pleases John, whose first book it is, and who is smarting from reviews which contrast it unfavorably with Jim Kunen's *Strawberry Statement,* whose counterpart *Kumquat* admittedly is. John's account of the phone call is rendered as Buster Keaton would have done it, dry face, slightly cynical, but clearly pleased; and we tingle with the thought that there is probably not another editorial office in New York City that would appreciate a congratulatory telephone call from Spiro Agnew."

It was a heady experience, and others quickly followed. That winter I met Agnew during a taping of Buckley's "Firing Line" show, at which he gave my book a big plug. Later in the year, I attended a luncheon for Agnew and a number of corporate leaders at Buckley's home. Agnew insisted that I sit beside him, which required moving a prominent industrialist to another table. And after lunch, during a question and answer session, Agnew strongly recommended that the assembled corporate leaders read my book. Again, a heady experience.

That summer, I went to Washington as a consultant on Agnew's staff, and in August he asked me to stay on permanently as a speechwriter. And that was the headiest experience of all. A spot on Agnew's small personal staff was one of the most coveted in Washington among young conservatives, whose numbers were swelling. He was, we believed, the most important national politician of the decade. And it was increasingly likely that he would be the presidential nominee—and the winner—in 1976.

Everyone was somewhat startled, therefore—including me—when I said no. I had been offered a teaching job at Arizona State, I told him, and wanted to accept it. So we went to Trader Vic's, drank navy grogs, and said what was to turn out to be a temporary good-by.

I don't know today precisely why I said no. It wasn't easy. I wanted the job, and my wife wanted me to take it. Despite a few minor reservations, I continued to admire Agnew greatly, and hit it off well with the members of his staff. Nevertheless, there was a warning buzzer, faint but persistent. It had nothing whatsoever to do with bribes or kickbacks—few of Agnew's staffers, up to the last day, ever thought such things possible. Nor was it quite Agnew himself, although after the short stint on his staff some doubts about the way he did things had begun to grow—having his barber driven from Baltimore to his office, for instance, or calling in his tailors to the office to fit him out with a new set of suits, often just before a visit to Frank Sinatra in Palm Springs.

But those were just symptoms. Let me give you a very small example of what made me uneasy. On my final day on his staff that summer, a secretary brought me a generously inscribed picture of Agnew. "You're very lucky," she told me. "He signed it himself."

A picayune example, to be sure, but it says a great deal about the White House milieu and the men who move in it. It is a high honor to receive a personally signed picture, and it is considered that the signer has made an extraordinary effort to sign it, as if he had just punched his own elevator button, a task usually reserved to Secret Service men. In most cases, however, the principal is spared such tasks. In the matter of signing pictures, for instance, the standard practice is to use staff forgers for those recipients who carry some weight. For the rest, there's an automated stylus called a robo-pen, which duplicates signatures and which is often used in conjunction with a computerized typewriter that can produce thousands of apparently personal letters, composed by mail specialists on the correspondence staff. Thus, if you write to the White House on an important issue, and if you receive a signed reply, it is almost certain that your reply has been composed and written by machine, and it is even more certain that the man to whom it was addressed has never seen your letter.

This is not meant to be an essay on the robo-pen. It is, however, an attempt to describe what makes many of us uneasy about White House life. And it is a way of life that Agnew seemed to cherish.

There were, I believed when I first met Agnew, incredibly important things going on out in the country, a clash between ideas and ideologies, the resolution of which would have profound effects on the shape of our society. Yet it seemed impossible to understand fully the significance and sharpness of this clash, given the insulation provided by White House packaging and protection. The daily lives of our top officials are arranged down to the minute by their scheduling staffs. They are briefed on the issues of the day by assistants who boil everything down to a few concise pages, a dangerous procedure if those assistants want their bosses to consider only certain options. There are aides whose job it is to insure that on trips there's always a change of presidential or vice-presidential underwear on hand. There are military aides whose primary function it is to escort the presidential and vice-presidential ladies at important functions. There are aides to relieve them of the plaques, dogs, rugs, blankets, Indian headdresses, cowboy hats, Shriner's fezzes, and pom-pom girls they are customarily presented with when traveling. There are secretaries, pilots, Secret Service agents, doctors, barbers, houseboys, cooks, Filipino messboys, maids, musicians.

There are the middle-level managers—Domestic Council, Office of the Management and Budget, National Security Council—who, sometimes with and sometimes without the cooperation of the departments and agencies, actually make national policy, which they then explain to the officeholders. And there are the speechwriters, whose function it is in part to translate those policies into coherent English so that Presidents and Vice-Presidents can read them to the nation.

It was this army of insulators and image burnishers that Agnew was asking me to join in that summer of 1971. Many of my reservations were the obvious ones, most of them having been much written about recently under the heading of "The Imperial Presidency"—or for that matter, the Imperial Vice-Presidency. I also said no for other, less tangible reasons. That summer, for instance, I shared a handsome office with several other Agnew staffers. The office had once been occupied by Black Jack Pershing, and it was simply wrong that several bright young men and I should be filling his space. There was something wrong with all those lavish appointments, for which the American people foot the bill. There was something wrong with the very existence of a staff interior decorator, who'd do your office to order. There was something wrong with the bright young men whizzing around Washington in government cars. There was something wrong with a White House staff of over five hundred people, the majority of whom did nothing substantive whatsoever. There was something wrong with the good salaries and fringe benefits and the luxuries as rewards for doing little more than writing memos, talking on the telephone, and moving papers.

That was part of it. But even more important was the nagging suspicion, only partially understood, that I'd be giving up something very important if I accepted that job. I had been a free spirit during that summer as a consultant. But if I went to work for Agnew on a permanent basis, I'd be his man, for in Washington the best staffers are extensions of the men they work for, and those who insist on remaining their own men have a way of disappearing rapidly. If I accepted that offer, I sensed then—only partially, but sensed it—I'd be giving up a part of myself that I might never get back again. And I was right, of course, but I didn't quite realize what I meant then.

And so, on that final day, Agnew took me to Trader Vic's, we drank several navy grogs, and it seemed that some sort of small personal circle had been satisfyingly closed. It had begun at Berkeley and at Trader Vic's in San Francisco, had curved from New York to Washington, and was closing back on a western university campus.

Fitting. And I wish I'd left it that way. But I'd forgotten what daily life in the academic world can be like, and although I didn't realize it, I'd been bitten by that little bug endemic to Washington, and was soon to break out with a low-grade but persistent case of Potomac fever. Finally, in June of 1972 it became unbearable, and I returned to Washington just in time for Watergate and the campaign. From then until the resignation, I was Agnew's man.

What was he like? I've spent a good deal of time since 1971 thinking about that. And the answer, I fear, is that I just don't know. I should know, of course. I'm not unobservant. Further, as his speechwriter, I was actively engaged in creating the appearance that should in some way have corresponded to the reality beneath. But I'm not sure it ever did. Before I came to know him as well as most staffers could know him, I thought I knew him very well indeed—so well, in fact, that I confidently wrote a book in which I analyzed the way his mind worked. But it seemed to be that with Agnew, the more you knew about him, the less you knew him. And that may explain everything.

There were, of course, the obvious things. He was quirky, with an almost consistently offbeat way of looking at things. Some of this I see in retrospect. After his resignation, for instance, we met for lunch at Sabatino's in Baltimore, where a friend, moved to something close to pity by Agnew's plight, offered him, for his own uses, a small educational foundation. We spent much of the meal discussing what he could do with it, wincing whenever he mentioned his pet idea—a series of seminars for businessmen at which the participants would discuss problems such as bribery. And months later there was even more wincing when he chose to use the foundation to publish a newsletter with a strong anti-Israel slant. Typical Agnew, those of us who had worked for him agreed.

He had, he maintained, finely tuned political instincts, yet the politicians he picked as winners seemed invariably to end as political losers. He was, for instance, one of the most fervent supporters of Nelson Rockefeller's comic candidacy in 1968. (Perhaps surprisingly, he still says today that he wishes Rockefeller had become President.) He believed, at first, that the Des Moines speech, which made him, had destroyed him. And at a party in 1976, he carefully and at great length explained to me why only Lloyd Bentsen had a chance at the Democratic presidential nomination.

He thought of himself as a fine administrator, yet his office, always oddly structured, was, after the campaign of 1972, a shambles. He elevated an unqualified secretary to the position of assistant chief of staff, and she, together with Agnew's own secretary, supervised the day-to-day operations of the office, arbitrarily assigning people to jobs they couldn't handle, terrorizing the secretarial staff, demoralizing the rest of us.

This was the aftermath of the Haldeman purge, during which Agnew had been ordered to cut the size of his staff by 20 percent. He had every reason to refuse. He had just completed a highly successful national campaign, during which he had added significantly to his already substantial personal constituency. Polls showed him the leading contender for the Republican presidential nomination in 1976. He was, in short, a force within the Republican party, with an independent base, and thus in a position to assert his independence. Further, we believed at the time, he was a tough man, a fighter. But when the word came to cut the staff, he obeyed without a murmur, purging several of his oldest and most loyal retainers, all of whom felt brutalized. Later, a White House aide who had been with Richard Nixon when Agnew was told to make the cuts reported that Nixon had been startled at Agnew's easy acquiescence. "The Vice-President," Nixon is supposed to have said wonderingly, "is a very soft man."

This was also the period of Agnew as Queeg. We checked in when we arrived, checked out when we left, and checked in when we came back from lunch. The lunch rule was rigidly enforced. We were expected to be back at 1:30 P.M. on the dot. Periodically, Agnew's chief of staff, followed by a military aide with a clipboard, would burst into the office at 1:31 P.M., taking the names of those not present. Anyone still at lunch, no matter what the reason, would later be called into Agnew's office to explain to the Vice-President of the United States why he had trouble getting back to his office by 1:30 P.M. Once there was a line of staffers waiting outside the office to make their explanations, and several of us compared the scene to Captain Queeg's strawberry hunt.

Agnew was a finicky man. At some point during the campaign of 1972, he suddenly seemed to become bored with it all, still relishing the trappings, but apparently tired of campaigning. This sudden attack of ennui, combined with a certain obsessive quality that had always characterized him, led to a period of excessive nit-picking. At one point, for instance, he discovered the comma splice and from then on seemed as obsessed with the search for comma splices in his speech drafts as he had been in scrutinizing university hiring policies for instances of quotas. Later in the campaign he discovered the split infinitive and once, having unearthed one, threw his speech draft half the length of the campaign plane.

"At least," I said to Herb Thompson, then the chief speechwriter, "he's finally make it up to the S in his grammar book."

This obsessive quality intensified as the troubles mounted. Shortly after his resignation, Suzy Cox visited him in his transition office across from the White House. After some strained conversation, he asked her suddenly: "Do you ever read the dictionary?" "Well yes," she replied. "I use it quite a bit." "No," he said. "Do you *read* it?" He then pulled out a yellow legal pad on which he'd been copying words and quizzed her on their meaning. He had, apparently, been systematically working his way through the dictionary, from A to Z, copying out interesting words.

There are numerous other examples of compulsive behavior. Yet most effective leaders are compulsive—Jimmy Carter, for instance, insists on personally clearing anyone who wants to swim in the White House pool. In fact, we value idiosyncratic traits in our leaders, frequently viewing them as what Dickens called "eccentricities of genius." We also expect, however, that these eccentricities spin out of something larger. And here, as I came to know Agnew better, was where the problems arose. That fascination with words, with well-constructed sentences, could have sprung from a genuine latent scholarly bent. Or it could have been fed by a desperate desire to impress. The same could have been true of his late-life attraction to ideas. He developed, for instance, a great interest in the writings of Irving Kristol, and during the last year one of his obsessions became to have boiled down in some usable fashion a slim volume by Kristol called *On the Democratic Idea in America.* Suzy Cox tried it, and for months she came at it from every conceivable direction. She reviewed it; she summarized it as a whole; she summarized it chapter by chapter; she isolated the themes and explicated them; she wove the themes together and summarized them. But after each effort his secretary would call Suzy to tell her that that wasn't what he wanted at all, and a few days later she'd call again, reminding Suzy that "the Vice-President wants his Irving Kristol material." Finally we decided, rightly or wrongly, that all he really wanted was to be able to talk to Kristol in his own language, and that somehow he just couldn't do so on the basis of his own reading and analysis. He may have been one of those admirable men who come to ideas late in life and are riveted by what they have missed. This is the way I thought of Agnew when I first met him—a self-educated man, like Eric Hoffer, who suddenly discovered the world of the mind and typically became an enthusiast. And it is true that his best speeches—especially the early ones—are highly intellectual efforts. But later I discovered that he had a minimal amount to do with the writing of those speeches, and during the campaign of 1972, when the only speech he fretted about was to be delivered to a Conservative party gathering in New York, where he would share a podium with William Buckley, the suspicion grew that he was primarily interested not in the intellect but in impressing intellectuals.

And this, in the end, may have been all that the man was really about. The impression he made on others was all-important to him. He was not interested in people; he was interested only in how people viewed him. This may explain why there remains such confusion today about his alleged involvement in petty political corruption. Each of us who came into contact with him saw him as we wanted to see him. His was a remarkably compartmentalized life. There were his show business friends, for whom he liked to shine as a celebrity. There were his Maryland friends, for whom he was the successful protégé. There were his staffers, for whom he played the sage leader. And toward the end, there were the intellectuals, among whom he increasingly shone, just before the troubles began, as an intellectual diamond in the rough. He was, in short, precisely what we all wanted him to be. He seemed to have great presence, an appearance of solidity and strength, although it startled many of those meeting him for the first time that in person his appearance—the narrow shoulders, the hint of gawkiness—was substantially less solid than the image captured by the camera. In private he could be crude, but in public he seemed always to move within an aura of decency and righteousness. Once, shortly after the Democratic Convention in 1972, I watched him stagger around his office, waving his fingers in the air, doing an imitation of Tom Eagleton undergoing electric shock treatments. Later, on the same day, he came to a staff party and gave a little talk in which he admonished us all never to make fun of that unfortunate man, Eagleton. "Isn't he *nice,*" said one of the secretaries.

Agnew's composure in public was impressive. There seemed always to be a strong sense of something quiet and profound, something indwelling and ingathering, a very private and very tranquil center. But perhaps that peace and tranquility, that apparent indwelling, was something else altogether. Perhaps there was nothing there at all—or perhaps what was there was small and shrewd and watchful, waiting for us to supply whatever it was we most wanted to be there.

Norman Mailer, attempting to understand what it was about Agnew that so impressed, concluded that it was "the symbol of his appearance"—just that and nothing more. There was indeed a presence. But perhaps it was a presence of our own creation, much as an actor is in part the creation of his audience, existing only as what we perceive him to be rather than as what he is apart from our perception. Agnew was something different for all of us. To the members of the New Majority, he was morality incarnate, come to put down the insurrection and cleanse the nation. To his enemies, he was the great fascist beast, a Mussolini or Perón intent on bringing down the repression. Yet in the end, he was neither.

The charges against him, and his failure to attempt to refute those charges, made it impossible for him to continue to symbolize morality. And the pettiness of the offenses with which he was charged disbarred him from playing Satan. He may not have committed those crimes the Justice Department accused him of committing. But by choosing to plea-bargain, and by copping a plea, he gave the appearance of having committed them. And since "the symbol of his appearance" was everything, the results destroyed him more thoroughly than a run-of-the-mill politician would have been destroyed.

Agnew's one great gift—persuading us that the appearance we chose to apprehend was also the reality—is to some extent shared by most successful politicians. But if it is *all* appearance, when that appearance is no longer correlative, then the gift is that of the con man or the actor. And in the end, it may have been as simple as that—Agnew may have been a great actor, riding a tremendous streak of luck.

As Vice-President, his reputation had nothing to do with what he *did*, but rather with what he said and how he said it. He wanted to prove to the world that he was a man of talent and ability, but the personification of talent and ability in his view was Frank Sinatra, and he made few attempts—even when the opportunities occasionally presented themselves—to play a substantive role in the administration. When he talked about leaving politics, he fantasized about going into television, becoming a celebrity, and making money. He was bored by the duties of his office, but relished the ceremonial aspects, as any frustrated actor might, and he valued above all the contact it gave him with celebrities like Sinatra. He seemed intent on proving to those celebrities that he was one of them, an entertainer himself. He loved to hear audiences laugh, to be thought of as a funny man, and to that end we leaned heavily on the services of a former Bob Hope gagwriter, who fed us a steady string of one-liners. Frequently he seemed to value those Las Vegas–Hollywood jokes more than the speeches he read, and he could be put off his feed for days if they didn't come in on time.

The central role of luck and the lack of center in his career is striking. He became governor of Maryland only because of a fluke split in the Democratic party, which left him appearing to be the only acceptable liberal in the race. As governor he seemed both liberal and conservative, expanding poverty and pollution programs on the one hand, putting down rioting blacks on the other. The latter activity drew Nixon's attention, but he was picked primarily as a compromise candidate, of those available the least likely to make waves. He made them, however, and during the campaign many believe that his fluffs nearly lost the election. As a result, he remained for a time

Spiro Who, in the White House doghouse. But then came Des Moines, and the luck was running again.

The Des Moines speech on the responsibilities of the media, called by one nonconservative columnist "the greatest sustained polemic in the English language of the 20th Century," was strictly a White House operation. Richard Nixon, stung by the instant analysis of his national televised speech on Vietnam, ordered that it be given. The words and ideas were supplied by Patrick Buchanan, Nixon's chief conservative speechwriter. Angew's role was that of leading man—he was to read those words in a convincing manner, which he did splendidly. It was one of the great performances in American politics. But, ironically enough, he didn't want to give that speech, which overnight made him the voice of the Silent Majority. And when he had finished that speech that night in Des Moines, he told an aide that his political career was obviously over.

I don't know now how I would have reacted had I known when I first met Agnew that in Des Moines he had simply been reading another man's words, and reading them with reluctance. But I do know that I would have viewed him very differently and would never have become his man. Later, when I did become his man, I came to view him somewhat differently. But by then it was too late. I didn't realize at first, as most Americans don't realize, that the majority of national politicians seldom have anything to do with the words they read in speeches and frequently don't know what they'll be reading at all until they begin to talk. Nor was I quick to come to grips with what this meant, probably because it was during the campaign of 1972 that I first allowed myself to think about it all, and it began with a very small incident.

In 1972 Agnew functioned as the Administration's chief campaigner, traveling 43,972 air miles and speaking in fifty-six cities in thirty-six states. It was a grueling campaign, and as it wore on, the heckling began to pick up. At first, Agnew countered it by pulling out a silver whistle and blowing it at the hecklers. (The whistle had been given to him by one of the TV camera crew, who blew them whenever they saw a pretty girl.) But the word had spread, and soon the hecklers were bringing their own whistles and blowing back.

It had begun to throw Agnew off stride—despite that unflappable exterior, it was surprisingly easy to throw him off stride—and he asked us to come up with something that would give our supporters in the crowds sufficient reason to shout the hecklers down. So that morning, on the flight from Washington to Wilmington, Delaware, I wrote a fast, little essay-lecture on the necessity for civility in a democratic society. It was typed up on the speech typewriter, a machine that types only in large capitals, and inserted behind the text of the speech to be delivered in Wilmington.

The heckling began almost as soon as Agnew had delivered two of the opening one-liners. As it picked up, Agnew flipped to the rear of his text and read the essay-lecture on civility. The crowd loved it and shouted down the hecklers, and the press was impressed, for it seemed spontaneous.

James Wooten of the *New York Times*, a reporter not given to lavishing praise on conservative politicians—or for that matter, politicians of any stripe—wrote about it in this way. "It was Mr. Agnew at his rhetorical best—establishing a simple premise, expanding it to broader, more philosophical planes, moving to a terse, sharp conclusion—and those who had come to hear him loved every word."

But the problem was, I realized that it was actually *me* at my rhetorical and philosophical best. It was Agnew at his reading and acting best. And that, perhaps, is the quintessential speechwriting problem. We are they. Or they are us. Or perhaps, essentially, it's just that they aren't they. "It's the greatest job in the world," one of the best of Agnew's former speechwriters told me. "You just write whatever you want to say and he reads it."

That was something that I didn't want to believe. Nevertheless, it's difficult indeed for me to sit here and tell you I was duped, for as a speechwriter and ghostwriter, I was actively engaged in helping to construct the appearance that passed for reality. And it would be disingenuous for me to pretend that I didn't realize something was basically wrong, once I joined the Agnew staff. Nor can I deny that I stayed on after realizing that something was indeed wrong. But it's difficult to shed illusions, especially when those illusions involve ideals and you have personified them. You start with the ideals—certain moral and social views that inform the way of life you want for yourself and your family—and, especially in times of great stress, when those views are under assault, you seek out a national figure—Spiro Agnew, as he appeared in Des Moines—who seems to personify those beliefs. If you're a speechwriter, you write sentences that lay out those beliefs, he reads them, and as you listen, you are convinced you're working for a man of principle. You and he *agree*. Why else would he read those words?

Nevertheless, if a speechwriter can't make the distinction between the rhetoric he writes and the reality beneath it, if he can't realize that he's creating an empty and artificial context, then the general public has very little chance indeed. Perhaps politicians should not be allowed speechwriters. Perhaps there should be some test devised to disqualify from running for office any man incapable of explaining himself to his constituents in his own words. Perhaps Walter Lippmann was right.

"A public man," wrote Lippmann, "can and needs to be supplied with material advice and criticism in preparing an important address. But no one can write an authentic speech for another man; it is as impossible as writing his love letters for him or saying his prayers for him. When he speaks to the people, he and not someone else must speak. . . .The truth is that anyone who knows what he is doing can say what he thinks. Those who cannot speak for themselves are, with very few exceptions, not very sure of what they are doing and of what they mean. The sooner they are found out, the better."

In contemporary politics, however, it has become nearly impossible to find them out, given the retinues of insulators, packagers, and image makers. And the tendency to personify makes it even more difficult, a tendency that will exist for as long as there are emotionalists, moralists, reactionaries, and Irishmen.

After Agnew's resignation, William Buckley warned against this tendency. "We go to such lengths to identify positions with people that we find it hard to detach those positions from those people when it becomes convenient to do so. So comprehensively did Agnew emerge on the political scene as the incarnation of law, order, probity, and inflexible ethics, that now that he has fallen, we are made to feel that the case for law, order, probity, and inflexible ethics has somehow fallen too: that ethics itself is subject to bribe and delinquency. This tendency to anthropomorphize our ideals is an American habit that can get us, indeed has just now gotten us, into deep trouble."

That is, I am sure, precisely right. Yet it is difficult to see, in this and similar instances, how this sort of personification, this identification of positions with people, can be avoided. Nor is it a uniquely American habit. In times of great stress and high emotions, in times of revolutionary ferment and civil strife, people in all nations tend to seek out leaders who personify the principles for which they struggle. And this was true of the America of the sixties. It is, no doubt, preferable to choose public men solely on the basis of their position on the "issues." But when the issues are intangibles, as they were in the sixties—and as they were during the last presidential election—it is difficult indeed not to personify. A man can take a stand on a set of issues such as defense spending, abortion, or busing. But he cannot take a convincing stand on those less tangible issues such as honesty or decency or morality. Everyone, of course, unless a candidate of the Satanist party, says he "stands" for such things. But the only way he can prove it is to personify them, to live them in his daily life. The job for us is to attempt to discover whether he does so, and that is a formidable and frequently an impossible task.

We believed Agnew personified those qualities. True, there were a number of warning signals, but we needed him, for he not only said the things we had been waiting for a national politician to say, but seemed also to supply the missing dimension within the Nixon context. Most of us thought of Nixon as a very shrewd and very tough politician. But few of us viewed him as the most moral man on the political scene, and we had no doubt he'd bend an ethical code whenever necessary. Agnew, however, seemed to fill the bill. As Jimmy Carter seems to many to personify the New Testament qualities of love, charity, and forgiveness, so Agnew personified for us the Old Testament concepts of justice and vengeance. (The parallel is an interesting one. Both men awakened and played upon emotions. Carter beat out his Democratic rivals not because of his position on the issues—few knew what they were—but because he appeared, alone among the Democrats, to personify intangibles such as love and faith. Like Agnew, he offered a missing context. One hopes that in this case, appearance resembles reality.)

In the end, it is partially our fault for personifying in Agnew those values we were seeking to defend. But he allowed and encouraged us to do so, and because of the gap between what he pretended to represent and the reality beneath, he cannot be judged leniently. One can make relative judgments about the behavior of other politicians. Senator Kennedy, for instance, is largely forgiven for Chappaquiddick just because people perceive him for what he is, and despite certain ludicrous performances, such as his speech explaining his heroic postcrash swim, he seems to make no special attempt to convince us that he's something he isn't. Agnew, however, cannot hope for similar tolerance. It isn't available to a man who celebrated the absolute, but pleaded *nolo contendere*.

CHAPTER FIVE

"IF a writer has had an unusual experience likely to interest a good many people, he has an instinct, and perhaps even a duty, to write about it." Stewart Alsop, *Stay of Execution.*

"People tend to forget that my presence runs counter to their best interests. And it always does. That is the one last thing to remember; *writers are always selling somebody out."* Joan Didion, *Slouching Toward Bethlehem.*

It was an unusual experience, and in evaluating it, I find that my feelings about Spiro Agnew run deeper than I realized. They are not gentle feelings, but there's nothing I can do about that. Nevertheless, given old associations and past loyalties, I'd be remiss if I failed to make the case for Agnew as many of his friends still see it.

You might, for instance, look at many of the character traits I have described from a slightly different angle and come to totally different conclusions. Agnew was, without a doubt, quirky and somewhat eccentric, and although I am convinced those quirks and eccentricities would have made him a very chancy President, they might also be viewed as admirable manifestations of individuality in an Administration not believed to prize individualism.

He was easily bored and largely uninterested in the duties

of his office, true. But that may have been inevitable. He was, undeniably, an intelligent man, and he occupied an office with substantive duties capable of challenging that intelligence. A Vice-President's only real job, after all, is to wait for the President to die or get carried off.

He was not a good administrator while occupying that office. But that may have been only because there was nothing much besides people to administer, and he was not interested in people as such. In Maryland, however, where there had been a coherent governmental apparatus already in place, he was generally given high marks for streamlining that apparatus and manipulating it effectively. He was good with things and the way they ran, and although people as people didn't interest him, he frequently seemed fascinated with what they did and how they did it. He recognized excellence when he saw it and was often able to put it to his own uses.

Nor is it easily proved that his interest in ideas and intellectuals was wholly superficial or self-serving. There are powerful and well-developed ideas in his early speeches, for instance, and although those speeches were written for him, he recognized what was in them and chose to deliver them. At times this led to trouble, as in the case of one writer who saw nothing at all wrong with lifting impressive sections out of other speeches without acknowledgment. Thus, if Agnew wanted to sound Churchillian, why not just borrow, word for word, from Churchill himself? There's certainly no better way to sound authentically Churchillian.

This practice came to a halt when Herbert Thompson and Dr. Jean Spencer took control of Agnew's writing operation, and it didn't happen again. Nevertheless, the fact that it happened at all may be instructive, especially if you want to make the case for Agnew as late-blooming intellectual. He was naturally struck by the force of the ideas and the way they were expressed. But as a middle-aged man, just setting out to educate himself and in the process discovering ideas for the first time, it simply may not have occurred to him that these ideas had frequently been expressed before, and expressed well.

One often had the feeling that Agnew was a man mentally

thrashing about, searching for some way to break through into a different realm. How did you apply these ideas? What did you apply them to? Personal life? Career? Public policy? Government? Or perhaps you didn't apply them at all. Perhaps they were simply things to be worn and displayed, like all those tailor-made new suits. And then there was the good life that Agnew was also discovering, personified and epitomized for him by Frank Sinatra and Palm Springs. Was this life in any way related to the life of the mind, to ideas?

In the end, the two never came together. He ran out of time and luck, and now they probably never will. There was something incomplete in Agnew, something never realized, a sense of the need to aspire and succeed, but an inability to understand how or to what end. Agnew was not Gatsby. But there was something of Gatsby in him, and on the human level his fall was extraordinarily sad. And judged relativistically, in the way we judge most humans, Agnew does not come off as a villian. True, as he admitted in the courtroom in Baltimore when he pleaded *nolo contendere*, he was guilty of wrongdoing, at least in one year. "I admit," said Agnew, "that I did receive payments during the year 1967 which were not expended for political purposes and that, therefore, these payments were income taxable to me in that year and that I so knew."

Thus, the admission. He took "payments," and he did not report them to the IRS. Applying the relative measure, this is no mortal sin. Most of us have at least actively considered shaving the income we report. The IRS takes too much of our money, and the government puts it to many dubious uses.

Nor, if we judge Agnew relatively, is it difficult to understand why he took those "payments." When he took office, the governor of Maryland made $15,000, an astoundlingly small sum. (Until March 1978, thanks to the capriciousness of the Maryland legislature, the governor's salary was $25,000, while the lieutenant governor, the attorney general, and the comptroller all made $44,856.) Agnew had never made money, he had a sizable family to provide for, and he may have been a one-term governor with no future of note; there was nothing to fall back on in the bank account. Perhaps it was the chance to pad out that account a bit; perhaps it was the chance to pay some outstanding bills; or perhaps, and this seems most likely, it was the chance to live in the style that he believed was expected of him. This is something with which he seemed preoccupied, and he frequently complained, both as governor and as Vice-President, about being unable to live up to those expectations. Superficiality? Total preoccupation with appearance? Perhaps. But it might also simply have been a classic case of the second-generation syndrome, that belief common to immigrant families that success is measured by its surface expression. Second-generation children almost always have the central importance of making a proper appearance drummed into them. Especially in public life, it is usually the Jerry Browns, the upper middle-class children of well-off and well-assimilated parents, who feel secure enough to downplay appearances.

At any rate, the payoff apparatus was in place, it was a time-tested way of doing business in the state (and still is), and Agnew probably believed he needed money. No state contracts were awarded to incompetents, no one suffered, and several people gained. (There is a point to be made here. If we are going to pay our public officials less than a decent wage, and if they are not men of independent means, then something similar is almost inevitably certain to happen. And it has happened at one time or another in most states, the major difference being that the governments of those states, unlike Maryland and New Jersey, have not been subjected to intense scrutiny by zealous federal prosecutors.)

Moreover, in the area that causes most distress, there was no way in the world when it all allegedly began for Agnew to intuit that he would one day become Vice-President of the United States. True, if he continued to accept payments after moving to Washington, then the judgments—even the relative judgments—must be a great deal harsher. But among all the charges documented in the Justice Department's forty-page statement of evidence, the charge that he took payments while Vice-President is by far the most flimsily substantiated, depending as it does on the testimony of just one tainted man, fighting to save himself from jail. Furthermore, there is something about this particular instance, constructed very much like the kicker in a piece of fiction, which seems both too pat and too stagy, as if the prosecutors, aware of the weakness of their witness, wanted to shock us into accepting Agnew's guilt by playing on our emotions rather than appealing to our minds.

It is, in fact, the lack of a comprehensive and fully documented account of the Agnew case that has left great areas of doubt. So far, we have only the Justice Department summary, an incomplete and selective document, in effect a prosecutor's brief; and a book by Jules Witcover and Richard Cohen, *A Heartbeat Away*. The Justice Department summary rests almost entirely on the testimony of men out to save themselves from jail—which they did—and the Witcover-Cohen book is little more than a dramatization of that summary, the relevant sections written almost entirely from Justice Department sources—chief among them Elliott Richardson, Agnew's foremost political enemy within the Republican party. One gets the impression that the Justice Department opened every drawer, reconstructed every conversation, and handed over every relevant document to Witcover and Cohen in order to buttress their story. There is nothing wrong with this, of course, but it leads to a curiously one-sided account, and in many cases there are curious evasions.

In one chapter, for instance, Witcover and Cohen discuss in great detail the torrent of leaks to the press that began in August and continued until the resignation. These leaks obviously came from people with an intimate knowledge of the Agnew case, and each was perfectly timed, shooting the defenses out from under Agnew before he had a chance to mount them. The leaks seemed to be spilling from everywhere—the grand jury, the prosecutor's office, the Justice Department, the White House. As Witcover and Cohen pointed out, it was these leaks more than anything else that made it impossible for Agnew to come up with a convincing legal counterattack. He was, well before the last days, tried in the press and found guilty. The leaks, then, are a central part of the Agnew story, their source one of the most fascinating aspects of that story's plot. Yet Witcover and Cohen, while purporting to tell the whole story, refuse to discuss these sources. If they didn't know, this would be understandable. But the problem is that as one of the *Washington Post* reporters covering the case, Cohen was a primary recipient of those leaks. Thus, the whole story remains unsatisfyingly incomplete, and those who wish to judge Agnew relatively still have important questions.

Just what, for instance, was the White House role in forcing Agnew's resignation? It was a matter of common knowledge that Nixon wanted to dump Agnew in 1972 in favor of John Connally, and was prevented from doing so only because of the fear of a conservative outpouring of rage. Nixon had already compromised most conservative ideals, and dumping Agnew would have been the last straw. Did Nixon still hope to rid himself of Agnew and replace him with someone more to his liking? Or did he feel that Agnew's problems just provided an unwelcome counterpoint to Watergate, casting yet another dark shadow over an already suspect Administration?

What was the role of Elliott Richardson, the man who prosecuted the case, and the only man to take to the floor of the '72 convention to speak against Agnew's renomination? Richardson made no bones about the fact that he wanted Agnew out. Further, it was commonly believed in the White House that Richardson wanted the vice-presidency for himself. What was the role of Alexander Haig, who by the time Agnew's troubles began had become the prime mover behind the White House curtain?

No doubt the answers to these and numerous other questions will someday be culled from yet-to-be-examined White House tapes. Agnew himself promises to answer many of them in his book, in which he says he will tell the story of how he was driven out of office. And there is little doubt he was railroaded. But the question, of course, is whether he deserved to be, and whether it was better for everyone that he was.

There is one argument here that is not frequently made in print, but which nevertheless, given the times and the way

Agnew was viewed, has an air of plausibility. Some of Agnew's friends still do not believe that he was guilty of anything. He pleaded *nolo contendere*, they maintain, because he was backed into a corner by the White House and the Justice Department. Either cop a plea and walk out of the Baltimore courthouse, or fight it out and face a jail sentence.

Those who believe our jury system to be perfect would not, of course, see anything wrong with the second alternative. If Agnew were innocent, they'd say, he'd be acquitted. Perhaps.

But neither Agnew nor his remaining supporters took this alternative seriously. Agnew had been tried in the press by a relentless flood of leaks, they maintained. Anyone capable of reading without moving his lips would be intimately familiar with the particulars of the case and, barring advanced mongolism, would have arrived at the same opinion. And in Baltimore, where Agnew would have been tried, they believed that the opinion would have been that he was guilty. Any Baltimore jury, they pointed out, would be heavily black. And among Maryland blacks, Agnew was just about as popular as the plague.

It may seem on the surface of it a specious argument. But these Agnew supporters believe it. And further, the record shows that Maryland officials who come up against Maryland juries inevitably seem to end up being found guilty. The recent trial of Marvin Mandel is a case in point. The prosecutors had built a rambling, diffuse, and often petty case against him, one of the key charges being that he had used the mails for fradulent purposes by sending off the transcript of a press conference in which he allegedly lied to the University of Maryland. It was a peculiar case, one that even the most acute of the legal reporters had difficulty following, and the betting was that Mandel would either be acquitted or found guilty on a minor charge. But when the verdict came in, Mandel was found guilty on more than a dozen counts—many of them charges that the jurors admitted they didn't understand. Even Mandel, a Democratic politico highly popular in Baltimore, couldn't escape that hanging-jury syndrome. It's highly unlikely that Agnew would have done better.

There are also the other arguments. Many of Agnew's former Maryland associates and staffers still flatly refuse to believe that by strict definition he did anything illegal. The difficulty was not to persuade people to make payments, they say. Rather, it was to try to discourage them from throwing money on the desk. Further, they maintained, although Agnew did not report some of the money accepted as income, he and his aides did not believe it necessary to do so. To the best of their recollection, they insist, such money was spent for political purposes. As proof, they point to the fact even an IRS full-field investigation failed to uncover evidence that Agnew ever had a surplus of money to spend on himself.

The line between personal and political expenditures has always been a thin one, and there is a whole shady area here that tends to bedevil those politicians who do not keep meticulous books. Agnew's former aides may possibly be right, and it may have been partly a case of sloppy bookkeeping. And there could always be the matter of a basic misunderstanding of the illegalities of the payoff system. Contractors and engineers, after all, can and do contribute to Maryland political campaigns, and the fact they also get contracts for state work may have nothing to do with those campaign contributions. And if all or most of the most reliable contractors and engineers in a state contribute, the problem becomes even more complicated.

Because the whole case against Agnew has never been made public, and because Agnew himself has yet to argue his own case, these questions will continue to surface, especially among certain former conservative supporters, who loathe Richard Nixon even more intensely than did Dan Rather and therefore accept it as an article of faith that Agnew was framed by the White House for still unclear reasons.

But Agnew had his day in court, and he used it to admit, abjectly, to income-tax evasion. Not the most heinous of crimes, certainly. But if he did take payments and did dodge his taxes, then he wasn't the man we thought he was. Nor was the Agnew we knew the man who pleaded *nolo contendere* in Baltimore. The Agnew we knew would have fought it all the way to the Supreme Court, and the prospect of prison be damned.

I am told that in his book, Agnew intends to concentrate on the unfair treatment he received from Justice and the White House and will not set out to prove his innocence of the basic charges beyond a doubt. If so, the book will be fascinating reading for political scientists and those interested in devious White House machinations. And because his case was unique in American history, there will always be some measure of interest in all aspects of it.

But this is not what those of us who once so admired him as a symbol of something larger than ourselves want from him. The subtleties of his case, the process of his removal, are not what we want to hear about. We want him to persuade us of his absolute innocence. But that I doubt he is going to do, for if he could, he would already have done so. And despite its deficiencies, it was in its documentation of the web of payments during the Maryland days that the Justice Department report was strongest. Nevertheless, we all hope that he manages at least to refute the charge that he took payments in the Vice-President's office.

Whether he does or not is now moot, however. He was part of something that is dead, something that no longer has a context—and apparently never did. Everyone who once supported him feels sorry for his misfortunes as a man and admires him for the way in which he has managed to pull his life back together. Nevertheless, these things are extradimensional and have nothing to do with the Agnew we thought we knew. That Agnew no longer exists, if he ever did.

There are still moments when I see him against the backdrop of the past decade. I see him marching, stiff and slightly tilted to the right, into an auditorium to the tune of "Ruffles and Flourishes"; I hear the crowds roaring, "Say it again, Spiro,"; I watch him field questions with that remarkable surface composure. I remember how it felt to campaign with him in 1972, a campaign that we viewed as a trial run for the presidential campaign of 1976. I remember how pleasant it could be to have a drink with him, and I can still remember precisely how it felt when he called me for the first time to congratulate me on my book.

There are also those moments, especially when reading once-liberal magazines like *Commentary* or *Harper's*, when I am jolted by articles with distinct Agnewvian overtones. There is Tom Bethell in *Harper's*, for instance, assailing the media and in the process repeating nearly every point made by Agnew in Des Moines less than a decade ago. There is the *Public Interest* and, God save us, even the *New York Review of Books*, sometimes making the Agnewvian point. There is the new muckraking *Washington Monthly*, perhaps the best of its kind, often reflecting the sort of conservative cast of mind that once intrigued Agnew. The country is turning right, the pundits tell us today, and if these magazines and others like them are any indication, perhaps it is. And if it is, I realize at such moments, the Agnew we thought we knew would have been President today.

But those are the emotional moments, and when they subside there is nothing left except a vague sense of something very important missing. There may indeed be a new conservatism in the air, but if so, it is the property and concern of a new generation, and those of us who threw in our lot with Agnew have nothing to do with it. The whole Nixon administration, I am certain, paved the way for it. But it is not ours, and we forfeited our claim to it on that October day in Baltimore when Spiro Agnew revealed to us all that he was someone else.

CHAPTER SIX

THE period immediately after Agnew's resignation remains one of the haziest of my life. We had been given a month to find new jobs and clean out our offices, and the only thing that seemed important was to get through the day without thinking too much. People wrote résumés and updated civil service employment forms and frequently disappeared for days on end. The job offers came in—one from the Senate, one from HEW, one from HUD, one from Interior, but I neither went for the interviews nor filled out the incredibly detailed federal forms. Filling out forms seemed beyond my capabilities. Once David Gergen, Nixon's chief speechwriter, called to say that there was an office waiting for me on the first floor, and I was mildly flattered, for I seemed to be the only Agnew staffer the Nixon people wanted to hire. But I wasn't sure I wanted to go down there—or down anywhere, for that matter.

During Halloween week I went to a college in Michigan to spend a week in residence and give a lecture. I stayed up for most of that week, drinking and talking with the students, perhaps hoping to recapture some of that feeling I'd left in Berkeley in 1968. But it didn't happen, of course. The kids were just kids, the sixties might as well have been the Roaring Twenties, and all I got out of it was a terrific cold.

The night came for my lecture, which was to be given in a

packed auditorium, where many of the kids I'd met during the week seemed to be pulling for me. But the subject of the talk was "media bias," and as I struggled to get through all the old points that we had once made so fiercely, I found that I just couldn't finish. The words caught in my throat, stale words without savor or meaning, and I began to babble. It could, I suppose, have ended in a disaster of Lucky Jim proportions, had not a number of friends in the audience come to the rescue. And even so, it was bad enough. One angry faculty member stamped out, muttering. Later, he said to one of my friends, "That man is either drunk or crazy."

I took the cold back with me to Washington, where it developed into walking pneumonia, and I sat for several days in my office, sneezing and coughing and running an impressive fever. In the end, perhaps more than any other single factor, it may have been that cold that persuaded me to join the Nixon staff. I had cleaned out my desk, packed everything into cardboard boxes, and then spent several days looking at them. Occasionally I thought seriously about accepting one of the standing job offers and moving everything out of the building to a new office—or perhaps just home. But then I'd sneeze and cough, and the whole prospect of moving those boxes out of the building seemed as appalling as filling out a federal form. Finally, unable to come to grips with it all, I had the boxes wheeled down to the first floor and moved into a Nixon staff office.

I never unpacked those boxes during the remainder of Nixon's last year in office. Nor did I unpack them when the Ford people came in. That November, I was asked, as was Aram Bakshian, to move back up to the second floor to become Gerald Ford's chief speechwriter. We both refused, although I had been officially transferred to Ford's executive payroll, in large part because we shared strong reservations about the quality of Ford's staff. But I also had a couple of other reasons. One Vice-President a year was enough. I still had that cold, and I intended to neither unpack those boxes nor move them again until I left the building for good.

Toward the end of 1973, in the aftermath of the Agnew resignation, those seemed just as good reasons as any others.

* * *

"They love him, gentlemen, and they respect him, not only for himself, but for his character, for his integrity and judgement and iron will; but they love him most for the enemies he has made." Edward S. Briggs, seconding the nomination of Grover Cleveland at the Democratic Convention of 1884.

"Always remember, others may hate you, but those who hate you don't win unless you hate them. And then, you destroy yourself." Richard Nixon, final farewell to the White House staff.

* * *

His enemies were our enemies, and hating them was considered part of our job. For some White House staffers, it was an abstract sort of thing, growing more out of a loyalty to the institution of the presidency than loyalty to Nixon himself. Nixon, they believed, was under attack for ideological reasons by enemies who would gladly destroy the presidency if that meant getting him out of office.

Others saw it as purely political, a power play to railroad Nixon out of office, engineered by powerful Democrats on the Hill and in the law firms and think tanks that housed the Democratic government in exile. Still others viewed it as a variation on the same theme, but made the media the prime villain of the piece. And for a few, it was the last stage of the Civil War that had been raging since the mid-sixties. Perhaps there were new faces and new names, but it was still the same old enemy.

There were also the Nixon loyalists, people like Patrick Buchanan and Raymond Price who had been with Nixon from the beginning and whose personal commitment to him was total. And this commitment was not limited to the old hands. My office mate, for instance, Ben Stein, who came to the White House the day after I did, suffered from a case of genuine and passionate loyalty.

Then too, as is the case with any group of presidential courtiers, there were the charlatans, the mountebanks, the mercenaries, and the opportunists, many of whom scrambled rapidly upward through the White House command structure during the last days. You wonder, of course, why they wanted to. But it's nothing new with collapsing regimes. In Berlin they were still jockeying for position in the bunker right up to the last day.

Where do I fit myself into all this? I'm not sure, but I think my record shows I'm not an opportunist. As a fall-away Democrat I was never a passionate Republican partisan. The institutional argument left me cold, and it used to be positively embarrassing to have to write about related concepts like "executive privilege" as if they possessed some sort of a priori sanctity.

Nor was I ever a dedicated Nixon loyalist of the Ben Stein–Pat Buchanan variety. I couldn't be. For one thing, I didn't know the man. In fact, although we had met and exchanged words during the Agnew years, during the months I worked for him we had only one conversation, and that was a telephone conversation that lasted for just about one minute. Nor did that conversation invite passionate dedication. I had written a radio speech on education for him that he delivered, as he enjoyed doing, at some odd hour on a Saturday. After the speech he called me up. "That was a hell of a job, John," he said. "We didn't have anything to say, but you said it beautifully." Then he laughed and smashed his phone into the cradle.

We had no personal relationship, and I harbored doubts about him politically. Like many people in both parties, I viewed him as a gouging politician with some very peculiar traits and possessed of an inferiority complex of mammoth propotions. I voted against him in 1960, and had Robert Kennedy lived to run, I would probably have voted against him again in 1968.

Nevertheless, despite the quirks and the contradictions, I also believed him to be a man of great personal rectitude—and this was especially true after the Agnew experience. Also, I was firmly convinced that he had dealt kindly with Agnew by insuring that he was able to cop a plea and sidestep a stretch in the slammer. But perhaps most important, he was all we had left.

The context had finally narrowed down to comprise just one man. From 1966 to 1972 the people with whom I identified myself had fought what we viewed as a long counterrevolutionary battle. In 1972 we seemed to have won, and for a brief moment it seemed that we had swept along with us a great New Majority that would form a permanent new political alliance. But a little more than a year later, there we were, besieged and surrounded, everything we had been involved with for a decade suddenly bound up, apparently inextricably, with the political fate of one man. It was our own fault, of course. But by then it was too late. Whether we liked it or not—and whether we liked him or not—his enemies were our enemies.

Is it as simple as that? Probably not. I watch Dan Rather on "60 Minutes," and I try to remember what it was about the man that made me want to throw a paperweight at the television set. I watch Walter Cronkite on the evening news and find him positively benign and avuncular. I attend a meeting in Berkeley at which our former *bête noire*, Daniel Ellsberg, speaks against the neutron bomb, and I wonder how we were ever able to view this timorous, ineffectual man as the greatest threat to the Republic since Benedict Arnold. But then I watch yet another rerun of one of the Frost-Nixon interview segments, and some of it comes back.

It was a peculiar period, that last year, awash with great bursts of anger and zeal, followed by long spells of exhaustion and depression, our moods in large part rising and falling with the perceived fortunes of the man with whom we'd thrown in our lot.

It's not hard to recall the specific events—most of them peculiar events—of those last days. But it's much more difficult to remember what it felt like. There was an atmosphere, a rhythm that can't quite be recaptured, perhaps because it was so purely emotional, and it's as difficult to reconstruct an emotion mentally as it is to recapture a taste or smell. It's not easy for a writer to describe emotions; there frequently are simply no corresponding words, and we are forced to fall back on clichés. And in this case there's an added complication, for I'm not absolutely sure now that I felt the emotions I thought I was feeling then. I came to the Nixon staff immediately after the Agnew affair, which was for me the disastrous culmination of an emotional decade, and for weeks after Agnew's resignation I felt nothing but a strange, numb sadness, a sense of personal loss. Once I began to work for Nixon, the adrenaline came rushing back and the emotions seemed sharp again. But now I'm not sure they were my emotions at all. Perhaps I had become a burned-out case, substituting the Nixon administration's ups and downs for the lows and highs I could no longer quite feel personally. Perhaps I was feeding vicariously on the emotions that swirled through the White House compound during that year.

At any rate, whether direct or vicarious, it was a fine place for anyone searching for an emotional fix. Nixon was totally isolated, working hard in his office, we thought, before the tapes were made public. Those of us at the middle levels—and many at the upper levels—seldom if ever saw him during those days, and we depended on hearsay and the newspapers to find what was happening. There would be long, quiet, lethargic periods when nothing seemed to stir. The rhythm at such times was slow, heavy, somewhat depressing, with nothing much happening in the compound before afternoon. On these days Aram Bakshian and I took long lunches and left early to drink at the Press Club and explain to everyone there why they were wrong about Nixon.

This is not to say that there was no work to do during those dead periods. But it was mundane sort of work that presents no great challenge. There were the short "attack" speeches we wrote for those senators and congressmen still willing to defend Nixon and assail his enemies. There were speeches for top aides like General Haig and Anne Armstrong, and for various cabinet members who periodically flooded the country to sing the praises of the President's lasting structure of peace.

Then there were the lesser things, the sheer bulk of which may explain why the White House needs a sizable writing staff. There were the stacks of proclamations that go out under the President's name, commemorating everything from Labor Day to National Pickle Week. There were the potential press conference questions along with the suggested answers, the position papers, and the letters that require more than routine handling. There were the TV clips, the statements of support, the recorded messages, and a raft of minor things. During the Nixon-Ford years I wrote answers to interviews, articles for high school and college yearbooks, toasts, and a piece under one of my current leader's name for a Sunday supplement explaining why he loved his wife. There were book prefaces, ghosted guest columns, planted letters. And once, just before I finally moved my boxes out of the EOB for good, I was asked to write a short phone call for Ford. It began, if I remember correctly, with "Hello."

Also, during these periods, we were exhorted to attack our enemies and defend our President by such latter-day loyalists as Ken Clawson, the former *Washington Post* newsman who suddenly shot up through the White House chain of command during the last days to become director of White House communications. Several of us on the writing staff had been published writers before our White House tour and had continued to write under our own names. (On the Agnew staff it was forbidden, the theory being, apparently, that the appearance of your name in print somehow diminished the luster of the name of the personage you served.) Thus, we were constantly bombarded with material favorable to Nixon and urged, whether it came from Reverend Moon, Rabbi Korff, or Astrogologers for Nixon, to incorporate it into our own writing.

It was during one such period, with the Watergate tom-toms beating ever louder and the Clawson memos piling up, that drought hit the Texas onion fields and the great Onion Crisis of 1974 hit the nation. My colleague, Aram Bakshian, an epicure whose priorities are always in the proper order, tossed the latest pile of Clawson "attack" material into his wastebasket and proceeded to write a sentimental yet scholarly appreciation of the onion that was printed on the *New York Times* Op-Ed page, where it dwarfed the various Watergate analyses of the day. A minor matter, no doubt, but Bakshian's ode to the onion may just have been the best and most enduring piece of writing to issue from the White House in 1974.

And it did, much to the gratification of us all, puzzle those new super loyalists that a writer identified as special assistant to the President should be singing the praises of the onion rather than attacking our enemies. But writers, as we all know, are very peculiar people.

These were the dead periods. We loathed them when they were upon us, but frequently missed them when they weren't. For the writers, the single most frantic period follows the State of the Union Message, when the time comes to send the President's legislative proposals to the Congress. This is always a hectic time in the White House, but because of Watergate, it was an especially frantic period for us. Nixon had begun his second term determined to chop government spending and programs. A plan of attack was drawn up—the Battle of the Budget, it was called—and the troops were ready to jump off. But then Watergate intensified, people on the Hill began to use the words "impeachment" and "resignation" openly, the Battle of the Budget was called off, and suddenly we were fiscal friends to all mankind, ready to propose any program or spend any amount needed to dampen down that impeachment talk. Thus, the legislative proposals had to have something to please everyone and nothing to offend anyone. Furthermore, they had to be written in a way that would please the public at large and show the American people that their President was sailing along above Watergate, conducting the business of the people, for whom, of course, he cared very deeply.

On the face of it, the drafting of the President's legislative program for the year is a simple process. Under the Nixon administration, the drill was first to solicit fact, figures, and proposals from the appropriate departments and agencies in the executive branch. This material would be channeled through an organization like the White House Domestic Council (since renamed) and turned over to the writers, who would, with the help of White House experts, add some specifics, then translate it into English, get the necessary approvals, and send it all off.

In practice, however, it was an enervating, infuriating, and bureaucratically Byzantine process. First there was the original material itself. At the best of times, bureaucratic writing is dense, evasive, and frequently opaque. But this was not the best of times. Apart from the Defense, Treasury, and State departments, the bureaucracy was adrift. The Watergate tide was rising, and high-level bureaucrats throughout the executive branch were either mentally or physically jumping ship, or doing nothing at all, mentally or otherwise. Nor could we expect much help at the middle and lower levels, where several generations of Democratic political operatives-turned-careerists were waiting gleefully for the whole thing to sink. For despite the spate of news stories, the fact is that Nixon never approximated the success of his Democratic predecessors in packing the bureaucracy. Traditionally, each Administration has laid down a bureaucratic layer before going out, with political types taking a pay cut and reverting to civil service career status just before the new Administration comes in. No one was more successful at this than Lyndon Johnson. But then the Nixon administration departed prematurely, and before Ford left, career conversions were frozen. Thus, in comparison to the Kennedy-Johnson layer, the Nixon-Ford layer is very thin indeed, and the result is that the bureaucracy remains heavily Democratic.

Consequently, we found we could expect minimal help from the bureaucracy, where our friends were in large part either ineffectual or fuddled, unable to keep up with the current save-Nixon line, and our enemies were Democratic loyalists waiting for us to hang ourselves. Frequently, therefore, we had to start from scratch, creating proposals and in the process sometimes setting national policy as we went. A case in point: Noel Koch, deputy director of the speech department, asked me to work with him on the transportation message, in which we were expected to lay down proposals for a national transportation policy. This was a tall assignment, since we'd never had one before. And complicating it all was the fact that Nixon had decided to give a radio speech on that policy, which was yet to be devised. From a public relations point of view, the speech was a solid idea. Here was this beleagured President, supposedly preoccupied with Watergate, yet in reality interested in all aspects of domestic policy and eager to push forward with "bold new proposals," as political speechwriters like to put it.

Good P.R. But from a writer's point of view, it was a mess. For one thing, this was the time of the trucker's strike. If Nixon were going to talk about national transportation policy, he'd either have to ignore that altogether or say something intelligent about it. And either way, he'd make some enemies. And then there was the larger problem. We had nothing to say, and neither did the Transportation Department, which was supposed to be coming up with the basic proposals.

Finally, after a number of preliminary drafts with minimal Transportation Department help, Koch and I produced a draft with everything remotely pertaining to transportation thrown in. We mentioned clipper ships, we mentioned the pony express, we mentioned barge canals. Then Koch sent the whole thing over to Claude Brinegar, Secretary of Transportation, with a memo telling him that this was our national transportation policy, and that the President would present it to Congress and the nation as was—unless, of course, he wanted to contribute something.

He did, and came to our offices the next morning, arriving flushed and late. That night Washington had been smothered by the worst snowstorm in decades; there was no transportation, public or private, national or local; and Brinegar's limousine wouldn't start. Thus, the U.S. Secretary of Transportation had for a time been unable to get a ride.

We went into a conference room—Brinegar and an aide, a couple of Domestic Council representatives, Koch and I—and we hashed it out, with Koch doing most of the talking. Brinegar's best contribution, as I remember it, consisted of three key words, which he insisted we sprinkle throughout the text. "Say something about flexibility," he'd say. "Say something about balance. Say something about diversity."

And so, on that snowy morning, with minimal help from the Secretary of Transportation, a couple of Domestic Council staffers and two speechwriters formulated our national transportation policy. I'm still not sure we needed one, nor can I remember the details of what we came up with. But apparently it wasn't bad. When Brinegar finally resigned, Ford praised him in his farewell remarks for developing our very first comprehensive national transportation policy.

It wasn't always quite that bad of course, but the process, from beginning to end, was a frantic one, perhaps the single most enervating step being the last one, when every concerned entity finally initials its approval of the finished draft.

Inevitably, this would set off a round of squabbling within the Administration. Anything touching on economics, for instance, might be reviewed by the Council of Economic Advisers, the Office of Management and Budget, the Treasury Department, among whom there were frequent disagreements over the accuracy of figures. Each disagreement required that figures in the draft—and frequently whole sections of the draft—be revised. In the meantime, many of those figures would change, and as they changed the Commerce Department or the Labor Department or the Agriculture Department might decide they also needed to add some figure of their own.

Whatever the subject, there were always competing entities. Mention anything remotely connected with foreign affairs, and the State Department, whose writers are the most evasive and opaque in government, would insist on fudging up the relevant section, no matter how innocuous the statements. Then the National Security Council would want a look, as would the Defense Department, which seldom appreciated the State Department's prose.

Then, finally, there was the last-minute sign-off ploy, developed into a fine bureaucratic art by Richard Nixon's Domestic Council. Say you've been at it for a couple of weeks, rewriting and revising, changing facts and figures, and perhaps trying to soften some policy language sufficiently so that OMB and the Domestic Council will stop feuding and sign off on the text. By this time you may have run through twenty-seven drafts, everyone except the Domestic Council has initialed final approval, and the final almost approved draft has just been delivered by messenger. It's late—about 2 A.M.—and a few writers and secretaries are sprawled around the speech office. The secretaries are saying they won't type another word and they want to go home. The writers are saying they won't rewrite another page and they want to go home too. Suddenly, a Domestic Council type comes bouncing in. He has been watching the progress of that draft like a hawk, and he has been authorized to sign off for the Domestic Council—after just a few minor changes. Everyone groans. A few minor changes—that means the draft will have to make the rounds again. But what the hell, they really are small ones. So you make them on the spot, there's one final typing job, and then the draft goes in to General Haig. But these changes, of course, in terms of the way the bureaucratic competition would see them, weren't really minor at all, and a few days later the Domestic Council director will point out to General Haig that it was their input into the draft that gave it its strength an originality.

Somewhat frantic, to be sure. But this is the sort of thing that White House speechwriters are hired for. What made our operation very different from others, however, were the great emotional surges and retreats of the man we worked for. There would be the long, lethargic periods, and then a new mortar shell would crash into the compound—something like the eighteen-and-a-half-minute gap, for instance. (You may remember that General Haig, when asked his opinion of what caused it, opined that it might have been "a sinister force." From that time on, you'd see certain staffers wandering through the halls of the Executive Office Building, waving their arms wildly in the air. If you asked them what they were doing, they'd say they were trying to bat down that "sinister force." Later, when it was discovered that someone had been copying confidential documents near the speech offices and shipping them off to the press, we decided that the sinister force lived in the big Xerox machine on the first floor of the EOB. It stayed on with Ford, frequently tangling his tongue and tripping him. Under Carter, apparently, it moved up to the OMB offices and advised Bert Lance on his finances.)

The mortar shell would hit, we'd all be jarred out of our lethargy, and there'd be something like Operation Candor, launched shortly after I joined the staff. Nixon would suddenly break out of seclusion and whirl off on a campaign-style trip, designed to show the people he was still in there fighting, and the atmosphere became wild. There were the background papers to be written, fact sheets, speeches, brief remarks. Nixon liked them punchy—short, straightforward sentences, catchy phrases like "workfare, not welfare," and above all anecdotes, especially things we could invent that his mother might have said to him. These remarks would be written in the form of short paragraphs, Nixon would commit them to memory and deliver them without a text. Those who knew Nixon in the old days maintain that he once did this masterfully. But toward the end he seemed to be running these remarks through some mental garbler and they'd come out sounding increasingly unhinged.

Each of these operations was launched with great vigor and fanfare, and for a time the atmosphere in the compound was heady, with everyone talking about how well Nixon was doing. (By this, I fear, we meant that he had neither fallen down nor begun to gibber.) But then would come the disaster.

There was Nixon, hunched like Quasimodo and with a look of pure rage contorting his face, shoving Ziegler down an airplane ramp in full view of every camera carried by the national press corps. There was the totally incomprehensible incident at Robins Air Force Base in Georgia, when Nixon gibbered something at an air force sergeant who was holding up his son to see the President, something about being the boy's mother or grandmother. Then Nixon apparently slapped the sergeant and the boy began to scream, "The President slapped my Daddy."

We all had our own theories about the incident, but the consensus was that Nixon, curiously uncoordinated, with limbs and movements never quite in sync, and possessed of a totally inscrutable sense of humor, had lurched to a stop in front of the man to make an opaque joke. Seeing the joke had fallen flat, our theory went, Nixon then reached out to pat the man on the arm, missed, and hit him on the face.

Ingenious, no doubt. But there were numerous Nixon stories

set in the pre-Watergate days that made it at least plausible. According to one of them, a state trooper escorting a motorcade had lost control of his bike and was thrown, the bike falling across his legs and breaking one of them, Nixon, so the story goes, stopped the motorcade, stepped out, and asked the writhing trooper: "How do you like your work?"

Then there was the artisan who brought a nailess, intricately constructed, hand-carved chair to the White House. Nixon sat in it, it collapsed, and he fell on the floor. "How long did it take you to make this?" he politely asked the craftsman.

Nevertheless, during the last year many of the incidents seemed to involve a bit more than a somewhat awkward man who frequently failed to say the right thing. During a photo session, for instance, he asked the assembled newsmen if they had noticed that his face was somewhat puffy and his eyes red and swollen. Then he nodded, turned to go, and said, "Walnuts."

Later, a curious reporter closely questioned his doctor, who hemmed and hawed and finally admitted there was no affliction known as walnuts. Some time after, the doctor told the press he had looked into the matter further and had concluded that there may have been walnut trees growing around Nixon's boyhood home and he may have been allergic to them. Perhaps. But the problem was, there were no walnut trees growing around the White House.

It is, I realize, easy to do this sort of thing with Nixon. Not long ago, for instance, a *Daily News* columnists wrote that Haldeman was going to include in his book a scene in which Nixon takes off his clothes in the Oval Office, sits down at his desk, and asks, "What's on the agenda?" Johnny Carson picked the story up and used it in his monologue, and although the Haldeman book later proved to contain nothing resembling the scene, I'm sure there are millions of Americans out there who still believe it really happened. It's not hard to believe that sort of thing about Nixon.

How would we have handled a story like that in the White House compound in those days? We would have joked about it, of course, conjuring up all sorts of obscene possibilities. We always joked about those Nixonisms, real or imagined, and many of them would be acted out endlessly. But finally, after rounds of jabbering, I'm sure we'd have concluded that it just wasn't possible. Nixon walked on the beach in his dress shoes. Who could believe he'd take off his clothes in front of anyone?

We joked about these Nixonisms; but we didn't welcome similar jokes from outsiders. None of us really wanted to admit that the man we were working for might have cracked under the pressure, might have gone slightly bananas—or walnuts, if you will. And although we did laugh about it all, I don't think we really suspected that something was indeed badly wrong until we read the first set of released transcripts. We hadn't known what they talked about in there, or how they talked about it, but none of us had even the remotest idea that it was quite that bad.

Not long before the tape transcripts were released, during the period when Nixon's speech requests were becoming increasingly peculiar, he sent out word, cryptically, that he wanted more "truck driver's language" in his speeches.

I had worked with truck drivers, had once cooked in a truckers' restaurant, and suggested we begin a speech this way and send it in. "Ladies and gentlemen, it gives me great f...ing pleasure to f...ing be with all you good Republican f...ers in this great f...ing city."

But we didn't send it in, of course. Just another joke, and not what Nixon had in mind at all.

Later, however, we were to remember that peculiar instruction when we read the first transcripts, in which Haldeman, Ehrlichman, and Nixon seemed intent on talking truck drivers' language, although it never rolled as naturally off their tongues as it does at the truck stops. And it sounded much more obscene in the Oval Office.

We knew, of course, that they didn't talk like Allen Drury characters in there, but most of us were shaken by the aimless coarseness, the small and dirty preoccupations, the apparently conscious effort to demean and debase—and frequently, it seemed very much like self-debasement. And yet, even with this reaction, as if you innocently turn over a stone and find something slimy and unspeakable, I don't believe most of us were ready then—or are ready now—to see Nixon as the villain of the piece. For my part, after reading the tape transcripts carefully, I am more inclined to hold Haldeman and Ehrlichman culpable. True, he was the President and they were his men. But I believe he needed something from them, and they didn't give him what he needed.

What did he need? I don't know. I am not a pyschologist, nor did I know Nixon personally. But he was obviously an enormously complex man, and although his psyche has been probed and prodded by a host of journalists, historians, psychohistorians, and former staffers, none of them, I think have satisfactorily explained that strange brooding complexity that just may make Nixon the least understood and most fascinating national figure of his age.

I hesitate to add my own uninformed analysis to the rapidly growing stack of case studies, many of them undertaken by people with far more impressive credentials than my own. But suppose we were to start with a very simple premise. Suppose we begin by viewing Nixon as a man who fought his way to the top all by himself. He began as a poor boy, he clawed his way up to the House and to the Senate and to the vice-presidency. Dwight Eisenhower, then the most powerful man in the United States at one point had tried to shake him loose. But he held on, and after one defeat by a man who was born with everything he had been deprived of, Nixon, again all by himself, finally fought his way to the very top. It was, by any measure, a magnificent achievement, the epitomization of the American dream.

Yet something was missing. Along the way, he had made a host of enemies. You always make enemies when you claw your way up, especially when you do it all by yourself, and friends along the way tend to be very few. The American system offered the opportunity, and Nixon seized it. But he may also have paid the price—and that price is loneliness. And on one level, it may be just as simple as that. Perhaps Nixon was a very lonely man. Perhaps he needed someone outside his immediate family circle to be close to, someone with whom he could relax, someone who would admire him. Perhaps he needed a friend, and hoped to find that friendship within that small inner circle that had been established within the Oval Office. Perhaps, at last on top, he wanted to be one of the boys. But as the conversations show us, Haldeman and Ehrlichman gave him neither relaxation, nor respect, nor friendship. He still wasn't one of the boys. They interrupted him at will, they addressed him with no respect, they offered him no friendship. Instead, they addressed him and treated his suggestions with something that seems very much like contempt, much in the manner of underlings everywhere who suddenly discover something soft at the center of a once-dreaded superior. Nixon attempted to talk to them as an equal. But the tone suggests they didn't see it that way at all. Perhaps they interpreted that invitation to intimacy as a central weakness, a need that could be played on and used to turn Nixon into something that depended totally upon them. It's important, I think, to remember that despite the barrage of charges flying out of Watergate, it was only the attempt at covering up what was a relatively minor offense that drove Nixon from office. And the cover-up was directed from that small room by the members of that small inner circle.

"Of all the passions," C. S. Lewis once wrote, "the passion for the Inner Ring is most skillful in making a man who is not yet a very bad man do very bad things." This most naturally applies, of course, to those young Haldeman-Ehrlichman protégés who were to troop before Senator Ervin's committee. But it also just might apply to Nixon himself.

Since the discovery of the tapes, lawyers, investigators, congressman, Nixon staffers, and jurists have pored over them with the diligence of Talmud scholars and have come up with scores of contradictory interpretations. But although we can't always be certain of precisely what P said to H or E on numerous given dates, I think, if we read carefully, one thing comes through clearly in many of these conversations—P desperately wants the approval of H and E. And at times he seems willing to come up with the most outrageous ideas in order to win that approval. But they never quite give it, never quite let him be one of the boys.

I am convinced that they served him poorly, and I think the tapes prove that. Had they been different men, there may well have been no Watergate, or at the very least no cover-up. Given the nature of the contemporary presidency, with the inevitable isolation of the President, there will always be a tightly knit and secretive inner circle. And our problem is that there is no way in the world to insure that the members of that circle are men of high character.

But perhaps I'm going too far here. True, both Haldeman and Ehrlichman seem to have been men of defective character, urging Nixon on. And there is no doubt that the worst in Nixon was in part brought out by the structure of the presidency. But in order for the worst to be brought out as easily as it seems to have been brought out in Nixon, it must already be lurking there not too far beneath the surface, fed by a flaw of sufficient dimensions to allow the easy blurring of distinctions between the significant and the banal, the moral and the obscene, right and wrong.

What was that flaw? Again, I don't have the credentials to provide the answer. But there is something about that inner circle sitting in the Oval Office and talking incessantly and meanderingly—something about the quality of those conversations—that awakens a memory. There was a play by Sartre, very much in vogue in the fifties, called *No Exit.* The play was pure dialogue. Three characters sat in a room and talked. The furnishings of the room were Third Empire, a style that influenced the design of much of the furniture used in the White House. The characters didn't care much for one another, but they felt compelled to talk. And as the play progressed we realized that the characters were dead and the room was hell.

Each of the characters needs the other to sustain some central illusion about himself. The central character, a coward, uses his companions—in this case, two women—as mirrors, hoping as a result of what he says to them to see the reflection of himself he wants to see. He has no existence beyond that reflection, and according to Sartre's definition, when the only picture a man has of himself is that which is given back by others, then that man is dead.

This is, essentially, a simple statement of the philosophy of Existentialism, which many have said is the central philosophy of our age. If so, and if such terms can be used together, then Richard Nixon, suffering like the central character in *No Exit* from the quintessential existential flaw, may be the first tragic existentialist hero of our age.

But whatever the interpretation, and no mater how fanciful, there is no doubt that Richard Nixon destroyed himself, and he did so in that talk-filled room. As the psychologists have suggested, it was almost as if he wanted to. The tapes did him in, and he could have prevented that. Despite any number of semiplausible explanations, no one is quite certain why he installed them in the first place. No one understands why he didn't have them turned off when he discussed things like the cover-up. No one knows why he didn't destroy them, as Pat Buchanan and others urged him to do, before they officially came to be viewed as evidence. Faced with a series of choices, Nixon seemed inevitably to make the wrong ones, almost as if he were bent on self-destruction.

Nixon partisans will still maintain that Nixon was done in by those enemies he had been collecting since 1946, when he first went to Congress. And they do have a point, of course. His enemies were legion, many of them were well placed in government and the media. At the first hint of trouble they treated him much more harshly than they would have treated someone like an Edward Kennedy. (True, the press has been hard on Kennedy for Chappaquiddick. But then, his offense was a major one. In fact, some of his critics, among them Robert Sherrill, actually accuse him of murder. There is a distinct double standard at work here, the Nixonites believe, and they tend to agree with Lyndon Johnson's observation on Chappaquiddick. Said Johnson: "If I had been with a girl and she had been stung by a bumblebee, then they'd have put me in Sing Sing.") Further, there are those, and they are reputable people, who claim to have reason to believe that the whole thing was engineered by the CIA in cooperation with several other organizations.

Nevertheless, it's hard to get around the fact that he could have saved himself, but didn't. And perhaps that's just as well. He was elected in 1968 to calm the nation, to end the war in Vietnam, and put down the insurrection at home. He did this successfully, and by so doing carried out his mandate. And then, in the final explosion that he himself was primarily responsible for igniting, he cleared the air of a decade of hatred and bad feeling. That explosion also destroyed his presidency, and he took a lot of us with him. But perhaps that was best. Counterrevolutionaries are always troublemakers when the fighting ends, and they invariably stand in the way of the formulation of a new synthesis.

Nixon was an extraordinarily complicated man, and no doubt the country is better off without him. Yet those of us nurtured on the emotional turmoil of the past decade will miss him greatly, for things will never be quite that exciting again. He was the very last element comprising that sixties context, and with his destruction that context was also destroyed. The birth of the Free Speech Movement—1964; the death of the Nixon presidency—1974. It is seldom that a decade ends so symmetrically.

CHAPTER SEVEN

NOT long after Nixon boarded the last flight to San Clemente, an unpredicted torrential rain fell briefly on Washington. *Time* magazine brought out a special edition entitled "The Healing Begins." The Nixon pictures in the White House compound came down, and the Ford pictures went up. And Gerald Ford told us that "our long national nightmare is over." One unreconstructed Nixonite put it differently, however. "The Party's Over," he said. "Now, it's Bring on the Clowns."

For the first couple of weeks, nothing much happened, and then the heads began to appear, as they had on two earlier occasions. The first time was just after the election of '72, when all the Agnew staffers turned in their resignations. Our staff, we knew, was slated to be cut by 20 percent, although we didn't know who would be going, and we were to be moved out of our office into a smaller area on the other side of the building, to make room for Peter Flanigan's somewhat amorphous operation. So we sat, for several weeks, and then began the phenomenon of the appearing heads. The office door would open, and someone would put his head around the corner and look the office over very carefully, as if taking mental measurements. After a while the head would say something like, "Oh, excuse me," and then withdraw. The head, of course, was attached to the body of a Flanigan emissary. Later, after the Agnew resignation, as we sat out the last month in what was left of the vice-presidential offices, the heads began to appear again, this time belonging to Ford staffers and cronies from the Hill. And now, down on the first floor, I sat among my already packed boxes and watched the heads begin to appear. During my months with Nixon I had kept a large photograph propped up against the wall. It showed Agnew, wrapped up in a black raincoat on an overcast day, scowling and squinting as he reviewed an honor guard of Portugese troops, with long bayonets attached to their rifles. (He looked very *right* there. Norman Mailer once attempted to come to grips with what it was that Agnew reminded him of. Typical politician? No. Businessman? Not quite. College professor? Obviously not. The suits, the grooming, the carriage—it was Juan Perón, Mailer decided, or for that matter any Latin dictator or the head of any Mediterranean junta.) The heads inevitably paused when they came to that picture.

For a time the heads appeared warily, and the lips didn't move. We were, of course, all under deep suspicion, the common assumption being that anyone sitting in those offices must have been in some way involved in bugging people, playing dirty tricks on them, and in general subverting the Constitution. Some of us, perhaps, could be rehabilitated. But it would require a lengthy period of intense denazification.

Throughout the compound, the purges of those publicly identified with Watergate and most of the new super loyalists began almost immediately. But the rest of us just sat and waited and watched the heads. Finally, one of them spoke. This head, from which the eyes seemed to protrude somewhat wildly, was attached to the body of Milton Friedman, an old Capitol Hill war horse who had become Ford's chief speechwriter after Bakshian and I had turned down the job. (That designation, while accurate on paper, is somewhat misleading. In the House, in the vice-presidency, and for the first part of his tenure in the presidency, Ford's chief writer was actually Robert Hartmann, a former newsman of legendary drinking habits who insisted on having the final editorial say on any piece of writing before it went in to Ford. And before the final days in the White House, when he was increasingly frozen out, Hartmann also did some of Ford's speechwriting from scratch.)

Friedman was an older man, amiable, a gangling sort of fellow with an odd loose gait who frequently seemed to be arguing with himself in the halls. Peculiar things were always happening to Friedman. One night, for instance, he fell asleep on his office couch and awoke to find a mouse running across his face.

Apparently Dave Gergen, who for the time being had been asked to stay on, had told Friedman that Bakshian and I were innocent of any Watergate war crimes, and so it was safe to talk to us. (This was true, and it was one of the reasons we enjoyed working in the Nixon speech operation. Early on, Gergen told the writers that they were free to turn down any assignment connected with the murkier aspects of the Watergate defense.)

Bakshian, Ben Stein, and I were, apparently, going to be asked to say on, at least through the transition (I was coming to loathe that word), and although both Bakshian and I had done a number of Ford's speeches, Friedman decided to offer us some advanced tutelage on the subject of writing for Ford.

Ford, he told us very seriously, suffered something he called "swimmer's breath," the result of which affliction, apparently, being an inability to make it all the way through a long sentence without drawing a shuddering gasp somewhere in the middle. Also, said Friedman, Ford was a very slow reader. So where it took, say, about ten to twelve pages of speech text to get Nixon through twenty minutes, Ford needed only five or six.

Further, explained Friedman, Ford had trouble with long or unfamiliar words or phrases, tending to get them tangled in his tongue. (Ford's problems with words were to become legendary, as when he mentioned the disease "sickle cell Armenia"; introduced Elliot Richardson as "Elliot Roosevelt"; referred to the "great people of Israel" in a toast to Anwar Sadat; praised the "ethnic of honest work" in New Hampshire; pronounced "holocaust" as "holy coast." Perhaps the single best one came at a White House breakfast, where he announced that Daniel Moynihan's successor at the U.N. "will follow the same policy of challenging some of the Third and Fourth World powers, calling a spade a spade." As one newsman put it, he might as well have said the jig is up in Angola.)

And so we wrote them short and simple. But the problem was that there wasn't much of anything to say, and for a time neither the writers nor Ford's advisers could come up with anything. Ford had brought with him to the vice-presidency a reputation for having one of the poorest staffs on the Hill, and during his first days it was the old Hill cronies who fed him advice. First came the gimmicks. We were going to Whip Inflation Now, Americans were urged to wear their WIN buttons, and Meredith Wilson was commissioned to write a "Win Fight Song," a scratchy taped version of which we listened to in the offices on one embarassing day.

Then, overnight, the emphasis changed. WIN buttons suddenly became inoperative, the belts we had been asked to tighten were loosened, and the President advised us "to take all we want, but eat all we take." Also, he suggested in a speech to the Future Farmers of America, it would be advisable for us all to take "a trash inventory of our homes." And that's just about where Republicans are today.

It wasn't Ford's fault, of course. After the sixties, after Watergate, after Nixon, there was simply no context left within which his presidency could sensibly fit. The Republican party was—and remains—a shambles, an empty structure without goals, policies, or coherent philosophy. In the fifties, when Eisenhower flatly refused to intervene in Indochina to relieve Dien Bien Phu (the First Marine Division in 1954 was on alert and ready to go), the Republican party was the antiwar, antiforeign entanglement, antiinterventionist party. But by the late sixties, the Republicans had become the most vociferous interventionists, with the Democrats, who had enthusiastically escalated the war, becoming the antiwar party. Traditionally, the Republican party had been the party of the budget balancers,which preached—and even frequently practiced—fiscal responsibility. By the seventies, as Nixon put it, we were "all

Keynesians now," and under Nixon, and then under Ford, we recorded budget deficits of such magnitude that Robert Taft must have groaned in his grave.

In social programs, the same transmutations occurred. Nixon outwelfared the Democrats with his Family Assistance Plan; both Nixon and Ford came up with proposals in education and health that were perfectly acceptable to many liberal Democrats. (Later, when he discovered the veto, Ford was to alter this course somewhat.) The Republican party had traditionally been the anti-Communist party. But there was Nixon trekking off to China, revering Mao as one of the magi, and then off to Moscow, to mime and joke and exchange nudges in the ribs with Leonid Brezhnev, the apparatchik who sent the tanks into Czechoslovakia. The Republican party had always thought of itself as the political repository of middle-class values—morality, honesty, decency—as opposed to those liberal Democrats whose only absolute was the absolute of change and flux. But then came Watergate.

Thus, when Ford broke out of the White House during the disastrous congressional campaign of 1974, and raced across the country speaking for every Republican in sight (many begged him not to come), he had nothing to say. Nor could the four of us who wrote his speeches manufacture a great deal. There just wasn't anything to say, and the man we were writing for didn't have a clue. We tried various approaches, the most dependable being to look over the transcripts of the speeches as given on the previous day, picking out those sections we had written that he used—and therefore, apparently, seemed to like—and working them into new drafts.

It was a frustrating, Mickey Mouse system, and compounding the frustrations of no input from Ford was the total lack of anything to say. We were told to be nonpartisan, since Ford was going to have to work with a heavily Democratic Congress, with the result that we seldom used the word "Republican" and never differentiated between the goals and philosophies of the two parties. (Perhaps that's just as well, since there's now so little difference.) Finally, in desperation, the theme Ford seized on was the need to preserve the two-party system, a theme that had been developed in an earlier unused speech draft by one of my colleagues.

The theme makes sense, of course. No one wants one-party rule. But as we laid it out, it sounded just a bit fatuous. Under one-party rule, we pointed out, massive abuse of power becomes possible. Therefore, in order to prevent potential abuse of power, it was necessary to send Republicans to Washington. But since it was a Republican Administration that had demonstrated to the country just how spectacularly power could be abused, the rhetoric had a certain hollow ring. It's difficult to say with a straight face that the only way to prevent future Watergates is to send men to Washington who represent the party responsible for Watergate. ("The Republican party is not responsible," said Ford, in one of his more memorable lines.) And the defense of the two-party system, while no doubt a noble idea, isn't the sort of visceral issue designed to stampede alarmed voters to the polls.

Then there was the problem with Ford's style. On the stump, he was an enigma. We wrote the speeches short and simple, careful not to trigger an attack of "swimmer's breath." But when he gave them, Ford suddenly seemed to develop a Fidel streak, rambling on at times for forty-five minutes, swimmer's breath or no, picking up some of the prepared remarks and garbling them, frequently breaking down into total incoherence.

The problem, of course, was perfectly understandable. Ford just didn't have anything to say and, in desperation, kept pushing against the outer limits of the rhetorical barrier, hoping that somehow he'd break through into some sphere of sense and ideas. But he didn't, and we kept thrashing around for new approaches, each one worse than the one preceding it. It was this frantic thrashing that led to the episode of the cards, and it was the cards that led to my first personal falling-out with the Ford people.

Cards. My problem with cards went back to Agnew. It all began with Agnew's speech notebook. The speech notebook, Herb Thompson had told me, was an old Agnewvian obsession. The idea was to write several comprehensive pages on every issue that he could conceivably be asked to address, then arrange the pages alphabetically in a loose-leaf notebook. Thus, say during a campaign, he could wait until the last moment before a scheduled stop, whip out three or four pages, and give a wide-ranging and spontaneous-sounding speech, astounding the audience with the breadth and depth of his knowledge.

The idea had simmered for some time on a back burner. But when I returned to the staff in 1972, just in time for the campaign, it had come to a boil. Agnew finally had three writers, and that meant he could finally have his speech notebook.

On paper, the idea doesn't sound bad. In practice, however, it can drive the people attempting to put it together walnuts. There is, for instance, the sheer bulk and complexity of the material you're expected to boil down. The inserts, we were told, should never run over three pages long. But it's difficult indeed to boil the economy down into three pages worth of flowing sentences. We had help, of course. On topics like the economy, for instance, the Council of Economic Advisers and the Treasury Department provided us with enough material to paper the White House, and sufficiently opaque and complex to confound a convention of Talmudic scholars—which, as ex-liberal arts majors, we definitely were not.

The three of us writing the inserts—Herb Thompson, Mel Grayson, and I—worked well into the night through much of the summer, fighting the campaign kickoff deadline, digesting material on everything from Abortion to Voluntarism, boiling it down, squeezing it onto three pages. Then the drafts would make the rounds to be cleared—our chief of staff, our political office, our military office, the Office of Intergovernmental Relations, the Domestic Council, OMB, the Council of Economic Advisers, the Treasury Department, the congressional liaison office, the National Security Council, and frequently to some of the most obscure nooks and crannies of the bureaucracy.

The people who reviewed our drafts were conscientious people, sometimes too much so. Someone, perhaps a Council of Economic Advisers staffer, would make a correction—the figure for current rate of unemployment, for instance. Then another CEA staffer would take exception to the correction and correct it. That summer, the unemployment figure was a particularly sensitive one. When we wrote our first draft, I believe, it stood at something like 5.5 percent. For the second draft, it went to 5.8 percent; for the third, 5.4 percent; for the fourth 5.6 percent. Finally, in October, when Agnew had predictably lost interest in the whole business, it became 5.5 percent again.

The easy thing would have been to settle on some sensible phrase like "approximately five and a half percent," since no one ever really knows what the real figure is anyhow. But Agnew didn't like to do that sort of thing. Few national politicians do.

As the drafts made their rounds, our own researchers would constantly nitpick us, appearing at all hours, asking, "Where did you get *this* figure?" The question would tend to send us into towering rages, since the suspicious figure would frequently be one that we had pulled out of the air to short-circuit the whole tedious process. At other times, one of our drafts—Old People, for instance (that was quickly changed to Older Americans, and for a time we flirted with Experienced Americans)—would disappear somewhere down on the first floor of the EOB for weeks. I recall going from office to office on the first floor one afternoon, asking with increasing irritation, "Who the *hell* is in charge of Old People down here?"

In the meantime, at staff meetings, Agnew would frequently frown, and ask after his speech notebook, as if he wanted to caress it. And periodically his secretary, who had a very sweet voice, would call to say, "The Vice-President would like to know how his speech notebook is coming." Agnew was very helpful about it all. "It'll take a lot of pressure off you during the campaign." he'd explain.

There came a time, finally, just before the campaign, when the end was actually in sight. We had made it down by then to Welfare or Women or some such topic. And then Agnew had another idea. Why not boil the three pages down into one-page outlines? Did that mean *throw out* those inserts? No, no. Just make outlines, one page long, and then devise a way to put them in the notebook so they faced the inserts . . .

So the process began again, with each outline also being routed for approval. And then, when the outlines were nearly done, Agnew had another thought. It might be even better if we boiled all those outlines down and put them on cards. Cards? Did that mean that we should junk the outlines? No, no, he explained. It's just that sometimes inserts come in handy and sometimes outlines are better, and sometimes cards are best of all—you know. We didn't, but we spent the next few weeks, humped over our typewriters, boiling down our boiled-down, outlined inserts, fitting them onto little white cards. (Art Sohmer, Agnew's chief of staff, told me that much the same thing had happened in the governor's office. Agnew had tried using cards there too. But on one occasion, after carefully arranging them for a speech, he had dropped them, they were shuffled, and he never tried them again.)

During the first week of the campaign, Agnew used the speech notebook two or three times, and expressed himself highly pleased, although some in the audiences seemed slightly puzzled when he threw together unrelated topics—Marijuana, say, Agriculture, and Welfare. Then one day he stopped using it altogether and we began to write an original speech for each stop, just as we expected to do anyhow. He also liked the cards, and was seen on occasion to fondle them. But no one ever saw him use them.

Two years later, we were sitting around the White House speech office late one night, waiting for someone to sign off on the congressional campaign speeches we had done for Ford. Suddenly the new chief speechwriter, Paul Theis, came bounding in. Theis, a smallish, quiet, gray-haired man with eyes that always seemed somewhat frightened, had been one of the numerous old-line Republican workhorses to come down from the Hill when Ford took over. He lasted for about a year in the job, then was sent to the Agriculture Department.

"We've got a great idea," he announced, and we shifted uneasily, for great ideas in the evening usually mean late night work that is discarded in the morning. "Let's try putting Jerry's speeches on *cards*."

Cards. I swore loudly, in what I fear was a very surly tone of voice, and stamped out. (I cannot remember ever having sworn at someone I worked for.) Later I was told that my reaction had understandably offended and annoyed Theis, who told a mutual friend that I seemed to be some sort of conservative hippie, something I had never before been called.

Later in the campaign I swore at Theis again, this time, ironically enough, over what may have been the single best speech of the campaign. Aram Bakshian, William Steponkus, and I wrote most of the speeches, which increasingly taxed our ingenuity. Part of the problem was the lack of anything to say. Another part of the problem was the channels through which the speeches had to fight their way to Ford. The latter problem began with Theis and ended with Robert Hartmann. Theis would fuss over drafts until the very last minute, crossing out anything remotely controversial and blanding them down until they were as innocuous as cottage cheese. Then, at the other end, there was Robert Hartmann, Ford's old adviser and crony from the Hill who guarded his position as final editor jealously.

Hartmann, whose drinking was a subject of constant conversation, frequently would call Theis late in the day to chew him out for some speech gaffe. And this is what he was doing when I swore at Theis for the second time. Sick of the bland diet, I had written an Agnew-style conservative stem-winder for delivery in Utah, where Ford would be speaking for the senatorial candidacy of Jake Garn. It had been a long trip and Hartmann had looked at the draft too late in the day to do much editing. But one phrase had jumped out at him, something about the bureaucracy being "jerry-built over decades." The point, apparently, was that someone would associate the "jerry" in "jerry-built" with Jerry Ford, and Theis had put in a panic call for me to come to his office to discuss the enormity of the implications. As he jabbered about it, the whole thing seemed so trivial and somehow extremely distasteful, and I swore once again, and once again stamped out.

Later, after Ford had given my speech as it was written, Senator-elect Garn told "CBS News" on election night that he thought it might have been that speech, more than any other single factor, that finally helped put him over the top. I was pleased, of course, since no other Republican in the country said that about any of the other speeches Ford gave for them. But by then such satisfactions seemed small indeed, just as trivial as the incidents that led to my swearing and the people involved in them.

By then it was clear that I would have to leave soon, either voluntarily or by invitation. One morning, I recall, a lady who was highly thought of by Ford and had been brought down from the Hill to help run the '74 campaign, sent out an emergency call. She was being interviewed by a group of journalists and wanted us to write an explanation for her of what Ford meant by the phrase, "veto-proof Congress." This was one of the key phrases in the campaign she was helping to orchestrate—we were fighting for the survival of "the two-party system," one of the reasons being that "one-party domination" would lead to a "veto-proof Congress." And vice versa. It seemed incredible that this key adviser and strategist didn't understand one of the few things said during the campaign that made any sense at all. But, in general, that's the way it seemed to be with the Ford people.

I had a four-martini lunch with a group of former Nixonites that noon, and in the afternoon I found that I just couldn't hit the typewriter keys well enough to write the lady's paragraph on the "veto-proof Congress." Nor did I care in the least, I realized. And so, for the first time, another writer had to pick up my assignment. That would have appalled me during the Nixon-Agnew years. But by late 1974, with Ford in the White House, it just didn't seem to make any difference. Once, when we all seemed involved in a civil war with the future of the nation at stake, even the silliest projects—making inserts, outlines, and cards, for instance—seemed imbued with at least a modicum of purpose and sense.

But after Nixon-Agnew, for many of us, that was no longer true. We were working in a caretaker Administration, presided over by an unelected President who could never on his own have had the nomination of his party. (And indeed, in 1976, despite the power of the incumbency, he very nearly made history by not getting it.) There was no real purpose, no programs and policies, no goals, no philosophical underpinning, no emotion, and it became increasingly difficult to write those senseless speeches, those silly jokes, the proclamations of National Pickle Week, those fudged-up signing or veto statements, those letters, TV clips, and telephone calls.

There was a great sense of drift in the Ford White House during those days, much of it the result of the hordes of people who wandered in and out, as Ford's advisers attempted to put together a staff. In the writing department, as in most other departments, the Nixonites were steadily purged well into 1975. (Later, as the White House geared up for the 1976 campaign, they were steadily brought back, Ford's advisers having belatedly discovered that many of them represented the best political Republican talent in town.) Their replacements were often odd types, men who had grown old in hack jobs on the Hill or in the bureaucracy with a surprising number of quirks. The Nixon writers, each of them, had been people of ability, competence, and talent, and each of them had a sense of purpose, even if misplaced.

But the Ford replacements were a different breed, frequently lending the whole operation an air of low comedy. There was the man from one of the agencies who one day, while rummaging around in his new office, came upon a man's black raincoat, in the pockets of which were a matchbook from a San Francisco topless bar and a pair of bikini panties. He burst into the secretaries' section of the chief speechwriter's office, waving the panties in the air, red faced, and shouting about morality. The secretaries laughed at first, thinking he was joking. But he wasn't. "A *very* strange duck," said one of them later.

There was the would-be writer who briefly occupied Pat Buchanan's handsome old office. He was assigned a secretary, young and attractive, who had frequently filled in for the regular secretaries in various writers' offices, among them Buchanan's. This older writing tryout spent a good deal of time wandering around near her desk, where he engaged in a peculiar habit. As he talked to her he'd unzip his trousers, then make various careful readjustments. Perhaps it was just an unconscious habit. Perhaps he had trouble keeping his shirt tucked in. But what ever the problem, it finally proved too much. He was bad-mouthing Buchanan, as he liked to do, and had gone through the zipper routine. The girl burst into tears. "At least," she sobbed, "Mr. Buchanan was a *gentleman*."

Stories of this sort floated through the early Ford White House. The guards of the Executive Protective Service, for instance, were horrified by the drinking habits of a trusted Ford aide, who, they maintained, was frequently seen in the morning drinking straight from a bottle he kept in a desk drawer. Apparently, according to the guards, he encouraged his secretary to do likewise, and one of them claims to have found her one morning, passed out on her office floor with her skirt over her head. There had been, as the world knows, bad things happening in the Nixon White House. But they were of a very different magnitude.

Later, after Donald Rumsfeld got a firmer grip on things, the atmosphere reportedly improved somewhat. But there were problems to the end, many of them the direct result of the quality of the staff. The writing department, consistently one of the best and most effective under Nixon, never recovered, and to the end most of Ford's speeches were at best banal and at worst embarrassing. Paul Theis simply wasn't up to the job, nor was his successor, Bob Orben, the right man. Orben was a talented and well-liked professional. But the problem was that he had made his reputation as a professional joke writer who had once worked for Red Skelton and had been originally brought to the White House to undertake the futile task of making Gerald Ford funny.

Orben was a decent man of considerable ability. But there is something about a professional gag writer working as chief speechwriter for the President of the United States that just doesn't wash, something that at the very least should drive political presidential image builders up the wall. During the primary campaign of 1976, several reporters with whom I had been traveling were passing around an ad, photocopied from the 1976 *Writer's Market*, a publication that solicits free-lance material. The ad read: "We are looking for funny, performable one-liners, short jokes, and stories that are related to happenings in the news. . . . The accent is on comedy, not wit. The ultimate criteria [*sic*] is, 'Will this line get a laugh if performed in public?' Material should be written in a conversational style. . . . We are particularly interested in material that can be used by speakers and toastmasters; lines for beginning a speech, ending a speech, acknowledging an introduction, specific occasions, anything that would be of use to a person making a speech." The address of the organization placing the ad was Washington, D.C. The name of the organization was Orben's Current Comedy and Orben's Comic Fillers. The editor was Bob Orben, also Gerald Ford's chief speechwriter.

This sort of thing never slips by the national press corps. And it's the sort of thing that rival politicians naturally love to pick up on. Said Democratic presidential candidate Fred Harris: "That's one of the reasons whenever the White House makes an economic policy it's a joke, and whenever they make a joke it's a policy."

Such cracks were predictable. And they were to intensify when Ford hired Don Penny, a stand-up nightclub comic, to help Orben make him funny. (Penny was later to take credit for playing a significant role in the speechwriting process.)

The writing operation, of course, is only one small part of the whole White House operation. But it can be an extremely important one, especially when the man you write for has no words of his own. If a President has no coherent overview of programs and policies, then the programs and policies of his administration will only be as effective and coherent as the ideas of the men who advise him. Similarly, if that President can't talk for himself, the quality of his public utterances will only be as good as the men who write them. And in this respect, a writing department can be the most important in the total operation, for the vast majority of Americans know their Presidents primarily through their public utterances.

Toward the end, Ford's advisers seemed to realize this, and began to search out talented people to help Ford get re-elected. And when they found them, they frequently also found that they were former Nixon staffers whom they had purged when they first came in. David Gergen is a case in point. Gergen, the last director of the Nixon writing department, had been purged in the most callous way possible. During a farewell lunch for a staffer at Trader Vic's, Gergen, who had spent long hours showing the Ford people the ropes, arrived late. He told us that he had found out he was fired from a wire service dispatch. They had told the press. But they hadn't bothered to tell Gergen.

This is not to say that they shouldn't eventually have replaced Gergen, or the rest of us, for that matter. But he did belong to the same party. And the way it was done said a great deal about the way the people closest to Ford operated.

Gergen eventually went to work for William Simon at Treasury. Later, however, with Ford in deep trouble in the primaries and the national campaign just ahead, they asked Gergen to come back to help out with the whole communications operation, then in a shambles. At first, however, they asked him to return very quietly and to let no one know he was there. He had no White House listing, no White House telephone, and for a time he worked furtively like some latter-day plumber, pulling the speech and communications operations back together as much as possible.

Toward the end, however, when the Nixon types began to return in a rush, and everybody knew it, they finally brought him out of the closet and named him director of White House communications. Ironically enough, as the Nixon people returned, it was the Ford people who were either being frozen out or leaving.

My turn came in the winter of 1975. Bill Steponkus, who had gone back to work on the Hill but retained close ties to the Ford people, called me to tell me I would soon be getting my walking papers because "someone over there" didn't like me ("Over there" was the West Wing of the White House.) I never found out who it was. Some said Hartmann. But others in a better position to know said it was Donald Rumsfeld, Ford's chief of staff. As soon as Rumsfeld arrived, they said, he did a thorough staff review and was appalled to find not just a Nixon holdover but an Agnew holdover still on the staff. If it was a public relations liability for a Ford speechwriter to have written for Red Skelton, it was even worse to have worked for Agnew. But whatever the reasons, it made no difference. It was time to go. As Victor Gold, Agnew's press secretary used to say, the elastic in my brain just wouldn't stretch any further.

I regret some things now. I wish I hadn't sworn at Paul Theis, for instance. He was a decent man trying to do an incredibly difficult job. But the swearing was symptomatic, having little to do with him and a great deal to do with me. There was simply nothing left, there were no longer any distinctions, just as there were no distinctions left during those conversations among P, E, and H in the oval office. Everything had become trivialized, and now it was all equally important or equally banal—boxes, messages to Congress, cards, bikini panties.

The temptation, of course, is to blame Ford for the banality of his administration and to laugh along with those critics who liked to call him "a dumb Nixon." But you can't call him dumb. No man who accomplished what he accomplished is dumb. Nor was it his fault that he inherited an Administration in disarray and disrepute. But there was something lacking there, something we have come to look for in our Presidents. That may be unfortunate, but it's a fact of American life. Ford was a smart and successful man. But he lacked some extra dimension. Nixon may have been searching for the self he wanted to be in the eyes of others. But Ford never seemed able to decide on what self he wanted others to see. Hence, his terrible image-building problem during the primaries, when the same Ford often never seemed to appear twice.

Nor did he ever successfully convince people that there was anything very much there beneath the surface. The problem with Agnew and perhaps Nixon was the great gap between rhetoric and reality. Yet we always knew there was something struggling in there. But with Ford it seemed to be all rhetoric, with nothing special at all inside trying to get out. And in

1976, this was a distinct political liability. People had had enough of politicians saying one thing and doing another. But they had also had enough of politicians whose rhetoric and actions had nothing much to do with anything at all. People were hungry for character and intelligence, with those qualities precisely reflected in rhetoric and a program for the nation. The time was ripe for a new synthesis, a new context, and the old establishment politicians like Ford had had their day, a day that will probably never come again.

I had become a functionary for those politicians, and the time had come to get out. I was asked to become Rogers Morton's chief speechwriter at the Interior Department, and accepted the job on a Friday. I was given an office, a secretary, and a special effort was made to dig a manual typewriter out of storage for me.

I went home that weekend and thought about it all—Berkeley, Chicago, the New Left, the New American Majority, the impudent snobs, the resignations. But it was all over now. There was nothing left, no context, just a few piles of ashes here and there, and several cardboard boxes sitting in my office in the EOB.

So, on Monday, I called Interior and told William Rhatican, an old Nixon hand and Morton's chief aide, that I just couldn't take the job. I'm afraid that I tried to tell him about elastic in the brain and the boxes and missing contexts. But he was very understanding. Then I drove into Washington, loaded the boxes packed over a year ago into my car, and went home.

CHAPTER EIGHT

THROUGH most of 1975 I stayed close to home, getting to know my family again and trying to sort things out. There were magazine assignments, speeches on a regular basis for several politicians, and a book. And once, late in the year, there was an argument with my wife. We had been to dinner and were beginning to talk politics again. Nineteen seventy-six, I told her, would be the year of the last hurrah for the old guard in both parties. Gerald Ford, the quintessential old Hill hand who had come to Washington in the forties, would square off against someone like Hubert Humphrey, another old-line Washington warhorse with roots in the forties. It would, I maintained, be a fitting way to end this wretched decade, with two stereotyped old political plugs plodding through what would probably be the last race of its type. She agreed, up to a point. She felt, as I did, that the end of Richard Nixon marked the end of one distinct era in American politics. But she also felt that there was something still shapeless stirring around out there, something that defied ideological labeling and shunned all the old tags. Ford, of course, would be the Republican nominee. But she wouldn't buy Humphrey, Kennedy, or any of the other comfortable Democratic old shoes. There was a new breed already on the move, she insisted, and the Democratic candidate would be Jimmy Carter.

I disagreed sharply. No one could tell the man from Terry

Sanford—Terry Carter, Jimmy Sanford. Carter, obviously, was just another one of those media constructs, beginning to get a build-up in the hope he'd knock George Wallace out in Florida. But that, of course, couldn't happen.

My wife would have none of it. Carter would win handily in Florida, she said, and his victory would signal the end of the period of American politics that began in the forties and concluded with the immolation of Richard Nixon. Then she took out a little red notebook and asked for my Florida primary predictions. That notebook has since mysteriously disappeared, but I gave Wallace about 33 percent of the vote, Jackson 26 percent, other potential candidates most of the rest, and Carter such a small percentage that I refuse to remember it. She wrote down her predictions, and we bet a dinner on it.

Later, after the Florida primary, I bought the dinner. Her prediction of Carter's total, made in *November 1975*, had come within two percentage points. Luck? Perhaps. But she did have an unfair advantage. I am a fall-away Catholic. She, however, is a born-again Christian of the Carter variety. There are, by conservative estimate, some 40 million of them out there. And while they're not all Carter enthusiasts, they seem to know things the rest of us don't know. And they have a terrific grapevine.

Nevertheless, I remained skeptical immediately after Florida. I still believed Carter to have been the beneficiary of a national media hypo and expected that he'd be dropped back into the pack after having carried out his primary mission of unhorsing George Wallace. And like most of the people who call themselves political observers, I didn't believe he could carry a major northern industrial state. But then came Illinois, which he won by a margin exceeding all predictions, the conventional wisdom was discredited, and suddenly we had all begun to talk about a first-ballot victory.

It was at this point that I found myself very much wanting to see the man, to listen to him and watch him in action. Television didn't do the job, nor were the speech texts or his autobiography satisfactory. But there was obviously something working there. He was playing profound chords, and they were striking deep responses in the people who heard him. But you just couldn't understand it, a number of newsmen told me, until you saw him live with a live audience. And even then, you probably wouldn't understand it. But you would feel it.

I don't know now, and I didn't know then, whether I wanted to feel it or whether I simply wanted to prove to my own satisfaction that it was just a new recipe for the same old-fashioned political moonshine. I like to think that by that time, after Agnew and after Nixon, I could look at politicians with detachment and objectivity. But no doubt that faint hope was still there. Like millions of other Americans, I was weary to the bone of politicians whose lives and actions bore no relation whatsoever to their rhetoric. However, according to many Carter supporters—many of them conservatives—and according to a surprising number of the newsmen who had been following him, Carter might just be the genuine article, a man of character rather than of created image or personality, whose surface was an exact reflection of what lay beneath.

This didn't seem highly likely, in view of the compromises that public men are required to make. Nor am I sure today, after watching Carter perform in office for a year, that it is the case. But it did seem possible, especially given Carter's religious commitment, a commitment that is infinitely more total and all-encompassing than most non-Evangelicals are able—or want—to believe. And if it were possible, then Carter just might be the new-breed politician who could construct that new synthesis, that new political context, on the ashes of a decade. There would be no place for me within that new context; but the thought that such a context might be possible somehow made the experiences of the past decade seem somewhat less futile. No doubt I was naive to feel this way. But it was a feeling shared by a number of conservatives whose lives had been touched by the Nixon-Agnew experience.

My first chance to watch Carter in action came in March 1976, when I briefly joined his primary campaign tour in North Carolina, on assignment for *National Review*. I didn't come away understanding the Carter phenomenon. But it was very definitely a phenomenon. Nor did I come away certain, anymore than I am certain today, that he is precisely what he appears to be. But I did come away convinced that Carter is very different.

In fact, the whole experience was very different. There was, for instance, the difference in the region itself and what its people seemed to be responding to. In 1972, with Agnew, we had crisscrossed the South, hitting all those "issues" like the three A's—Amnesty, Acid, and Abortion—the simple mention of which brought audiences shouting to their feet.

Our mentor was George Wallace, and in 1972, before the shooting, Wallace was still the South's roaring boy. He had sent that message to the established leaders of his party, and it had shaken them to their foundation; he had rolled up a huge popular vote in the primaries; and had he not been shot, he and his supporters might well have torn the roof off the McGovern convention. The Wallace constituency, that great group of exploited and ignored Middle Americans to whose understandable fears and frustrations Wallace spoke, was the envy of every strategist involved in constructing the New American Majority, and it was the Wallace constituency that Agnew assiduously courted, hoping one day to ride its votes into the White House.

In the wake of Watergate, however, all this seemed to have changed dramatically. Suddenly, almost as if it happened over night, the Wallace constituency had melted away. No doubt the health factor had a good deal to do with Wallace's inability to hold them. But it was more significant than that: The Wallace constituency seemed to have disappeared because the enemy had disappeared. True, the pointy-headed bureaucrats were still there. But with the collapse of busing and other social issues, they no longer seemed quite the same direct threat. And those college professors who can't park their bicycles straight were still among us. But in 1976 their campuses were quiet, no longer staging areas for Mustang-driving revolutionaries. Nor was there a great deal of point in 1976 in campaigning against McGovernism, for as the Carter surge suggested, McGovernism never became the force in the Democratic party that it had promised to be.

By 1976, Wallace had nothing left to attack, and Wallace not attacking was simply not Wallace. Nor did it seem that there was any significant number of his former constituents who were pining for a revival of those attacks. Wallace had suddenly become an anachronism, a man of the sixties most vividly remembered against a backdrop of social chaos. But that backdrop had been carried off to San Clemente, and Wallace had become a man out of his own time, a silent-screen actor without a voice for the talkies.

Two scenes from my trip to North Carolina stand out here. I had left the Carter tour after a huge rally in Winston-Salem. At the small airport, where I waited for a flight back to Washington, the word was that George Wallace, who had taken to following Carter from stop to stop, would be coming in at noon, and an area at the edge of the landing strip had been roped off for spectators. The Wallace campaign was in a shambles, the crowds had been falling off badly, and on this day there were no more than twenty men and women, mostly in their fifties and sixties, to welcome him. They were all working and farming people. Several of the men wore bib overalls, they all carried small Confederate flags, and there was a small country combo that sporadically struck up "Dixie."

Wallace's plane finally landed, two hours late. It taxied to within a hundred yards of us and stopped, and Wallace was off-loaded on the opposite side, so that we were unable to see him being carried down the stairs and lifted into his wheel chair. Then he was wheeled toward a motorcade waiting on the runway near the plane. The group stopped once, and Wallace gestured toward us. There was a brief discussion, and then he was pushed up to a limousine. His aides and guards clustered around him and the car door helped block our view as he was lifted into the limousine.

Then the motorcade pulled out slowly, passing within ten or fifteen feet of the ropes that held us back. The band played "Dixie," and most of the twenty people there pressed against the ropes, reaching toward the limousine. "God bless you,

Governor," someone shouted. "Give 'em hell, George." Wallace, his deeply lined face tight, rolled down the window and leaned out as far as possible, his arm outstretched, trying to touch those hands. But he couldn't quite reach them, and as his limousine turned the corner, he was still looking back, arm extended. The band played another chorus of "Dixie." But most of the small crowd had left before it was finished.

What had happened to Wallace? The question had largely been answered for me the night before at the Carter rally. The auditorium was packed with people of all ages and descriptions. First there was the musical warm-up by a young country-folk group called the Nashville All-Stars, country enough for the older people, but sufficiently with-it for the younger ones. As the time approached for Carter's appearance, they struck up a medley of three—first "Dixie," done soulfully; then "Battle Hymn of the Republic," done martially; and finally, "This Is My Country," triumphantly. Very neat, indeed—thesis, antithesis, synthesis.

The crowd roared, and suddenly, before you expected him, Carter was at the podium. The speech began immediately, like no other political speech I'd ever heard or written. There was no text, no cards, no outline, but instead an extended monologue totally devoid of the standard laugh lines most politicians demanded in their speeches. Carter seemed strangely motionless. Wallace used to bring them up roaring as he threw those overhand gestures, almost as if lobbing hand grenades. Carter, however, did little with his hands, occasionally raising them, palm upward. Wallace played the full range of vocalized emotions; Carter's delivery was almost without inflection, with strange pauses after certain words and phrases. After the musical build-up, you had expected the emotional pitch to continue to rise. And it did, but in a peculiar way. There was a great hush, an almost totally quiet, seldom broken by applause, the effect of that strange monotone almost hypnotic. Carter, it was obvious, gives off something. Critics call it self-righteousness; the more detached call it self-possession; but his Christian constituents call it serenity. And that night in Winston-Salem, it very definitely infected his audience.

I have thought a great deal about that speech and others like it that I listened to in 1976 in North Carolina. Our perspective on Carter has shifted since then. There are real questions raised by his performance as President thus far, and his administration seems inclined to take an arbitrary and sometimes slapdash approach to matters of policy, something that delights his natural political enemies. Further, with the saturation coverage that comes with the presidency, many of the keenest analysts and journalists who once found him fascinating are now probing into the psyches of new media favorites such as Jerry Brown.

This is natural. Our national attention span is short, and grows shorter. But it does seem just a bit unfair for those who praised him a year ago to be bad-mouthing him now. Nor is it quite reassuring to listen to the pundits discussing him as a one-term President before his administration has had a chance to get off the ground. And perhaps least reassuring of all are the comments you routinely hear these days—mostly from Democrats—that Carter is "boring." I understand that feeling of course. It's what makes me nostalgic for the sixties and for Nixon and even for the last days of Watergate. But is that really what most people want again?

I don't intend to attempt to defend Carter here. He is not my President, I didn't vote for him, and I doubt that I will vote for him—or for anyone else, for that matter—in 1980, although I may write in Eugene McCarthy's name. But for whatever the reasons—our disenchantment with politicians in general, our low threshold of boredom, our search for the new and bizarre—I suspect that we may be selling Carter short before we fully understand the man or what he may be offering to the country. For despite the pundits, who never gave him a chance at the White House in the first place and then fought against his nomination down the line, there are unplumbed depths that suggest Carter may yet emerge as a most formidable President.

Part of the problem at this early stage of the game is a basic confusion among those whose job it is to interpret Carter to the nation. In the end, like it or not, we depend heavily on the national media for these interpretations. But the media thinks of itself as "issue" oriented, and over the past decade the way the media deal with what they designate as "issues" has become increasingly stylized, increasingly divorced from the complex problems themselves. A politician, asked for his position on one of these "issues," has a number of stock responses to choose from, his choice generally dictated by party affiliation and ideology. The press expects to be fed one of these acceptable responses and expects to be able to interpret it in an accepted way. The problem with this is the problem with all clichés—eventually they lose their meaning and frame of reference, and code words take on a reality of their own, almost as if the words themselves, rather than some situation they were once meant to designate, are the real issues.

This, to a great extent, is what has happened to most of the "issues" of the sixties. Busing is a case in point. Once a politician need only mention the word to set off a whole string of connotations and reactions, springing from a deep and complex social concern. But suddenly, except for still-troubled areas like Boston, busing is no longer a national preoccupation, and thus a national politician can no longer mobilize a significant constituency by repeating the code word. And the same is true, despite very vocal single-issue minorities, of most of the "issues" of the sixties. But this is something that the national media didn't for the most part understand in 1976, nor do they on a large scale understand it today. Hence, the oddly dated quality of so much of the commentary on the nation's editorial and op-ed pages. For the Tom Wickers of the world, it is still 1968.

I understand that feeling, and I am also nostalgic—for different reasons, of course—for those days. But the fact is that all those "issues" beloved of the media are for the most part secondary problems. Some of them just naturally obsolesce; other are luxury issues—black studies, for instance. During the palmy days of the sixties, when the Vietnam War generated sufficient prosperity to provide a generation of protestors with scholarships and there were more jobs than applicants, black studies was a burning issue on the campuses. But today the money is gone, jobs are hard to come by, professors are competing wildly for a few available jobs, and things like black studies have become luxuries that few people any longer worry about.

No doubt somewhere down the road various of the now-dormant issues of the sixties will resurface. But in the wake of Vietnam and Watergate, they lost their primacy, for suddenly a *real* issued touched all our lives directly. Our government had become corrupt, our institutions seemed hollow, and our people were caught up in a spiritual crisis. It is no exaggeration to say that many Americans, although they wouldn't put it this way, felt that we were on the way to losing our souls, both nationally and individually. And it was to this issue, the only real one of 1976, that Carter spoke. And as he did so, he brought a whole new vocabulary of code words into the political dialogue, code words that the media simply didn't know what to do with.

Thus, that speech I listened to in Winston-Salem and others like it are really two speeches. In one part Carter touches upon the problems we call "issues." But that is the secondary part. In the primary part, he talks about character, morality, values, faith in God, truth, decency, forgiveness, love. Not the stuff that an issue-oriented press knew how to deal with in 1976 or knows how to deal with now. But to Carter's audiences, these words and concepts symbolize a whole system of values, a moral, ethical, and spiritual framework within which all "issues" will solve themselves.

In 1976, the other candidates spoke to problems out of context. Carter, however, dealt with the problem of the context itself. And that context is nothing less than the Christian religion.

This caused great confusion during the campaign, and continues to cause trouble today. "When you talk to a Udall or a Jackson," said one veteran Washington correspondent, "you know where you are. But Carter's like Gatsby. I don't know where he comes from."

Central to the problem, he continued, is "the whole God bit. It's culturally significant and provides him with a way of measuring things that people in Washington and New York aren't familiar with. And unlike any other national politician he's talking about value systems. He even has one."

He has indeed, and it seems impossible to understand Carter or his presidency without some understanding of the way that system shapes every aspect of his daily life. He prays scores of times each day, he tells us, and he never makes an important decision without praying about it. We have only his own word for this, of course, but I think we must accept it, for if he lies to us about his faith, then he is one of history's great scoundrels. And not even his severest critics quite believe that.

Early on in the primaries, a good deal was written about Carter's religion, some of it—especially the analyses by Richard Reeves—extremely valuable. But now, even as the pundits struggle to get a line on Carter and his presidency, the subject seems largely to have been dropped, almost as if it had been just another campaign ploy, something external, like a politician's image, that can be donned or doffed at will.

Why? Apparently it's just another of those things that doesn't fit. For one thing, the words and the concepts they denote aren't right. It's very seldom that you'll hear a national media man or a member of the Washington press corps saying, "Praise the Lord" or "Hallelujah" or "Thank you, Jesus." Nor will they often be caught seriously using words like "love." ("Compassion" is a word the more liberal among them can stomach, but it is used in a purely laic context, usually referring to what we should be feeling for those who live in ghettos.)

It is, understandably, a subject that most political analysts feel uncomfortable with, for to explore it could be extremely embarrassing. Carter, to put it into an inelegant phrase that is nonetheless familiar to every national media man, is a genuine, bona fide Holy Roller. That means he has been visited by the Holy Spirit. That means that he talks to Jesus on a daily basis, and Jesus talks to him. That might even mean, as is the case with his charismatic sister, Ruth Stapleton Carter, that he practices glossolalia.

The problem here is an obvious one. Few reporters are going to stand up at a presidential news conference and ask, "Mr. President, do you now or have you ever spoken in tongues?" Or, "Mr. President, did you speak with Jesus before you sent your welfare reform package up to the Hill?" It's just downright unnatural for a cynical and sophisticated Washington newsman to ask things like that. And what in the world would you do if the President answered both in the affirmative? What sort of story or column would that leave you with? And how could you possibly write it up or report it on television with a straight face? "President Carter said today that he has consulted Jesus on his welfare reform package. Jesus approves, the President said."

No. You couldn't do it. It doesn't fit at all. In Washington, until very recently, you just didn't discuss, at least for public consumption, certain idiosyncracies such as boozing or womanizing. The town has always crawled with boozers and womanizers. But you'd never learn it in the pre-Wayne Hays-Wilbur Mills period from reputable Washington newsmen. (At times, as when the tacit decision is made to attempt to bring a certain politician down, the women and booze stories will surface. But these have been the exceptions that prove the rule.) Nor, except when a politician makes a conscious attempt to raise the issue, as John Kennedy did in Texas, is the subject of religion discussed. It isn't hard to understand why. Few of the people who write and comment for a living in Washington are religious enthusiasts. Many of us are agnostics. Others of us occasionally profess, and for us there are the distinct and somewhat formalized systems of prayer and properly scheduled visits to the churches in which we do this praying. Religion, for us, has its properly and clearly demarcated role in the scheme of things, just like Monday night football.

The problem is this, however: If we accept all this as a blueprint for proper behavior and proper forms and subjects of discourse, then we are in danger of missing the point entirely. For most of those who have lived and worked in Washington, religion is one of these subjects, like booze and women, that is relegated to the sphere of private life. But as Nixon in the Oval Office and Agnew in the Governor's Office taught us, what a public man says and does in private may ultimately affect us all more profoundly than any of his public actions or statements. Perhaps, if we are to judge effectively the integrity and competence of the men we hire to manage our government, we must know about all aspects of their private lives. Perhaps we have a right to demand that a public man's private life be of a piece with his public posturings, and that he be forced to demonstrate to us that it is. Perhaps a public man has no right to a private life. Perhaps anyone who cherishes his right to privacy should be discouraged from entering into public life.

There are, of course, numerous problems here, not the least of which is the reluctance of the media to probe into what they see as the properly private parts of the lives of the public men they cover. At times, that reluctance can eventually get us all in trouble. And at times it can lead to misunderstanding and misinformation—or, as seems to be the case with Carter, an almost total lack of comprehension. Our opinion of our elected officials, of how they do their jobs and why they do them the way they do them, depends almost entirely on what we are able to glean from media reports. If the press doesn't understand the hows and whys, then neither will we, for few of us have the chance to cover the White House firsthand. And if the press refuses to consider the role religion plays in Carter's life and work on the grounds that it is a private affair, then they will miss what may be the central aspect of his presidency. And so will all the rest of us who do not share Carter's faith.

The fact is, as all born-again Christians will tell you, when you believe as they believe, there can be no distinctions between public and private lives. There is only one life and every aspect of that life is informed by faith. Your religion is your life and your daily life is your religion, as is your work.

This is not easy for those of us who are not believers of the Carter stripe to understand. Take the matter of prayer, for instance. Carter told *Playboy*, in that infamous interview, that he probably prayed twenty-five or more times each day. One Sunday morning, according to Robert Shogan's *Promises to*

Keep, he told the congregation at a Washington church that he had already prayed ten times. And one reporter tells me that he heard Carter say he prayed as often as fifty times a day when governor. Now to the nonconverted among us, the images conjured up by that statement are somewhat ludicrous. Does he suddenly leap up and scurry off to find some hidey-hole? Does he drop to his knees on a White House rug, as Woodward and Bernstein had Nixon doing?

Not at all, say his co-religionists. True, those prayer counts that Carter periodically issues are misleading. But he assigns a number to them for the convenience of the press, who probably couldn't understand it any other way. To understand it, they say, you yourself have to experience the special relationship with Christ that shapes the daily life of the born-again Christian. Especially as such a believer grows more mature in his faith they say, it becomes increasingly difficult to separate thought from prayer; normal thinking is in itself prayer, and when you think about a problem then you are automatically praying for help. Thus, they say, Carter, as a maturing Christian, would aspire to pray a good many more times than ten or twenty-five or fifty times a day; in fact, he would pray as frequently as he thinks. But how can he explain that to the rest of us?

This basic lack of understanding permeates most of the attempts at analysis of the Carter presidency. Recently, for instance, there appeared such an analysis by Hedrick Smith, Washington bureau chief of the *New York Times*, in which he tried to sum up Carter's first year. The Carter presidency, he concludes, is difficult to get a handle on, primarily because of what seem to be the contradictions in Carter's approach.

"Surprisingly," writes Smith, "for all his concern about organizational efficiency, Carter's White House staff is almost unstructured." Smith goes on to comment on the dearth of aides and Carter's tendency to function as his own chief of staff and policymaker, practices that we have not learned to expect from our Presidents.

Yet despite the inevitable confusion growing out of this one-man show, reports Smith, Carter seems well on his way to mastering the details of executive branch policies and problems in a way that few Presidents of this century have succeeded in doing. Is that good or bad? Smith isn't quite sure. He is deeply impressed with Carter's mental abilities, clearly superior to the abilities of recent Presidents. But the lack of advisers seems to trouble him, as does Carter's lack of interest in forging alliances on the Hill in time-honored fashion. Carter, he says, "comes across as a loner," and this seems to be, in Smith's view, the central problem thus far in his presidency.

To a born-again Christian, however, this is no problem at all, and should in fact be seen as a strength. At one point, Smith comes close to stating this view, when he quotes an unnamed cabinet officer: "Jimmy Carter is the kind of man whose strength comes from within, rather than from associations." But why does he possess that inner strength? Smith attempts no answer, and in fact ignores the whole subject. According to Carter's co-religionists, however, that strength is the manifestation of his faith.

Thus, from the Christian perspective, Carter cannot by definition be a loner, since he is never alone. Nor, by their definition, as long as he retains his relationship with God can he ultimately be wrong. There is, they believe, a divine plan for us all. Our job is to work as hard as we can within that plan—hence, Carter's single-minded attempt to master the minutiae of his office. If he masters the mechanics of his office, and if he stays personally in touch with God, then eventually, if they jibe with the larger plan, a way will be found to implement his policies and programs.

Farfetched? It still sounds that way to me, and it's certainly not the sort of thing about which a *New York Times* bureau chief would want to speculate. But it's not at all farfetched to Carter's 40-million-plus born-again co-religionists, who make up the fastest growing religious movement in the nation. And that 40-million figure is, if anything, on the low side, for it takes into account only white Protestants with relatively stable denominational ties. But the movement is much broader than that, including charismatic Catholics, Jews, and a substantial portion of all American blacks. It cuts across social, economic, and political lines. It is strong on campuses such as Berkeley, where the New Left once ruled. It includes young people and old people, longhairs and shorthairs, working people and professional people. Its members meet in all the established churches. They also meet in places with names like the People's Church or the Free Evangelical Church.

This born-again movement, like most movements that have sprung up during our lifetime, began in other parts of the country, and has only recently, despite a half-decade of rapid growth, begun to make it felt in the Northeast, where most of us were at first stunned and incredulous when people like Charles Colson and Eldridge Cleaver began declaring for Christ. But now even those of us who live and work in Washington realize that we are caught up in the midst of a genuine religious revival. Jimmy Carter in large part won the White House because of that revival, for although not all born-again believers liked his politics, the majority of them took him for one of their own. Carter owed his victory to other factors, of course, primarily the national post-Watergate blues. But just as his religion would have prompted the Democratic power brokers of the Northeast to deny him the nomination a decade ago, that religion in 1976 helped insure his nomination and election. And it may be that religion, more than any other single factor, that explains the man and his presidency.

This is not, as I have mentioned, a particularly popular view among those whose job it is to explain our Presidents to us. But recently there are signs that this may change, perhaps the most significant among them being Robert Shogan's observations in *Promises to Keep*. Shogan, who covers Washington for the *Los Angeles Times* and is generally regarded as one of the best national-affairs reporters in the business, was given carte blanche to roam the White House during the early days. He watched Carter and his aides at work, traveled with them, sat in on cabinet and senior-staff meetings, and came to a basic conclusion: This Administration, perhaps more than any other in recent history, is strictly a one-man show. Thus, Shogan believes, because this presidency is so much the function of one man's psyche, it is essential to understand the man, to get a feel for his character. And that, Shogan concludes, is not possible without understanding his religion.

There is a good deal more than speculation involved here. Shogan, who followed Carter through the primaries, is a first-rate reporter, and he thought to do what apparently has occurred to no other reporter in Washington—he went to the First Baptist Church, listened carefully to a Sunday school lesson Carter taught the congregation, and came away convinced of what he had increasingly come to suspect during his months of covering Carter. As he puts it, "It is impossible to separate Carter's faith from his Presidency."

Shogan doesn't quite understand that faith. His perspective and background, like mine, are radically different, and we share certain views of the effects of his religion on his character that his fellow believers insist are off the mark. "One of the most puzzling aspects of their faith to outsiders," writes Shogan, "is the apparent contradiction between the sense of self-righteousness that comes with being born again in Christ and the sense of humility that comes from the human awareness of human susceptibility to sin and temptation."

This, Shogan believes, is one of the natural tensions growing out of the faith that structures Carter's life, and he believes it helps to explain what appear to be important aspects of his complex character—both forgiving and judgmental, humble and self-righteous.

But those who share Carter's beliefs, while they agree that their faith causes natural tensions, don't quite accept the terminology. What we see as self-righteousness, they see as serene rightness, a quality that the rest of us have difficulty recognizing, simply because we have not experienced it. And they do have a point. Not only have we not experienced it, but we have seldom seen it in our Presidents, total self-assurance, to say nothing of serenity, being as uncommon in Washington as nonalcoholic punch.

They accept the humility side of the equation, and they agree with Shogan's thesis that Carter believes his single greatest problem as President is to resist the temptation to succumb to pride. This, according to the born-again view, could be fatal. Given his relationship with God, for as long as that relationship remains right, he cannot do anything wrong, for he is working within God's plan. But things would go badly wrong if he were to get out of touch with God, and pride could be the factor that puts him out of touch. A President is a very powerful man indeed, and with sufficient pride could begin to mistake God's design for his own—or even worse, his own design for God's.

No doubt this all sounds somewhat fanciful. It sounds fanciful to me as I write it. But this point of view does seem to beg for understanding. It is the view held by those who share Carter's very special variety of religious belief. And it is the view, they say, that informs his life and work. If so, then a basic understanding of Carter's religious beliefs answers a good many of the more troublesome questions being raised about the man and his presidency. Carter, it is said, fails to consult adequately with others; his administration is unstructured; he is too much of a loner; he is too concerned with detail; he can't take criticism. For those of us who are not religious, such criticisms seem sound. For a man who genuinely believes he walks and talks with God every moment of his life, however, they have to sound irrelevant. If he consults with God, then he must believe that advisers are somewhat superfluous. If his administration has been shaped to fit within God's plan, then organization charts are unimportant. If he believes his relationship with God to be right, then he needs no criticism, for what he does—whether it succeeds or fails—is determined by God's wishes.

I have, perhaps, dwelt overly long on religion here. But because it may well be the key to the Carter presidency, and because it has been so little discussed, it has seemed necessary to do so. Further, I believe that it is religion that explains why Carter appealed to so many conservatives in 1976. And it is religion that gave rise to so much of the ideological and political confusion that swirled around candidate Carter in 1976 and continues to swirl around President Carter today.

Is he liberal? Is he conservative? He may be neither or both, depending on how we choose to read the liberal-conservative evaluation charts that we have developed over the past few decades. In fact, he may even be a socialist. The problem is that we have come to expect stock positions on stock issues, defined over the past several decades. But Carter violates our expectations.

Consider, for instance, what many believe to be the definitive statement of Carter's philosophy of government: "There is no inherent conflict between careful planning, tight management, and constant reassessment on the one hand, and compassionate concern for the plight of the deprived and afflicted on the other. Waste and inefficiency never fed a hungry child, provided a job for a willing worker, or educated a deserving child."

Is that a conservative or a liberal view of government? To me it sounds like both, and it sounded like both to many voters in 1976. Yet perhaps it is well to note that two very different things are being dealt with here. One concerns methods, which sound conservative, the other concerns goals, which sound liberal. But without too much effort, "compassionate concern for the plight of the deprived and afflicted" could also be read as "Christian concern," while the methods described, "careful planning," and so forth, could just as easily be construed as socialist, rather than conservative, methods.

Does that mean that Carter is inclined toward socialism, as many of his more vehement critics assert? I don't think so, but it is not impossible, given his religious orientation. "Render unto Caesar," after all, if interpreted literally, precludes the acceptance of few contemporary systems of organizing society. Communism, of course, is beyond the pale, since communism is at war with God. There is no real reason, however, why a socialist nation couldn't also be Christian. Further, it should be remembered that the theologian Carter claims as mentor, Reinhold Niebuhr, was the founder of the Fellowship of Socialist Christians and one of the first Americans to call for "a Christian espousal of Socialism." True, Niebuhr later repudiated dogmatism, but it was from Niebuhr's dogmatic period that Carter gleaned his favorite quotation, one which he repeated throughout the campaign to explain his view of the mission of politics: "The sad duty of politics is to establish justice in a sinful world."

I don't believe Carter is a socialist. But I believe he could be without violating the central tenets of his faith. "Compassionate concern for the plight of the deprived and afflicted" is the social manifestation of Christian love. Like Niebuhr, Carter believes—if his statements can be trusted—that in society you must use governmental power to secure the ends demanded by love. Through that power you establish justice, and justice is the embodiment of love in the social structure. Therefore, since systems are mechanical things, you choose whichever one you believe will most thoroughly and effectively allow for the establishment of justice. And if that means socialism, so be it.

I don't believe for a minute that Carter would actually refer to himself or even in passing think of himself as a socialist. But neither is he a *laissez-faire* conservative. Most probably, if you could dissect his psyche, you'd find in the social section elements of both, plus a number of other things in between. And this may be the secret of his political appeal—an appeal that, in the last analysis, might most properly be called Christian, in the most all-encompassing sense.

In *Mere Christianity*, C. S. Lewis, who also underwent a born-again experience, speculates about what an ideal Christian society would look like: "If there were such a society in existence and you or I visited it, I think we should come away with a curious impression. We should feel that its economic life was very socialistic, and in that sense, 'advanced,' but that its family life and its code of manners were rather old-fashioned—perhaps even ceremonious and aristocratic. Each of us would like some bits of it, but I am afraid very few of us would like the whole thing."

Just so. And perhaps this was the secret of Carter's success in 1976, the same secret that may yet make him a formidable President. Very few of us liked the whole thing, or at least what we could see of it. But we liked those little bits we could recognize, some of them liberal, some conservative.

We chewed over those little bits, and as we did so, we liked to talk about "the new politics," of which the Carter phenomenon seemed the clearest manifestation. The "new politics," some of us hoped, would provide us with that new context that the nation so badly needed. But then it occurred to some of us that there might be nothing at all new about that context we were being offered; it might, in fact, be one of the oldest of the suprapolitical systems, and the "new politics" might be as old as Christianity itself.

In the end, this may be what drove many of us who had been fascinated with Carter's little conservative bits back to Ford. We liked those little bits very much and we appreciated a candidate who wasn't afraid to speak of absolute values absolutely. But we needed time to think before we accepted the whole thing.

CHAPTER NINE

MANY conservatives were intrigued with Carter in 1976, and many believed he might well prove to be a more conservative President than Nixon or Ford. There were a number of things to recommend him from the conservative point of view. As a devout Christian, he could be counted on to be constitutionally anti-Communist. As a firm believer in the afterlife, he probably could be counted on not to attempt to build the perfect society here on earth, although, given the Niebuhr influence, there was always some doubt about that. As an Annapolis graduate, he could be expected to take the proper position on national defense. And as a successful southern businessman, his instincts in fiscal matters would probably be conservative.

The basic appeal, however, was emotional, the perhaps understandable post-Watergate reaction to a politician who used words like "honesty," "integrity," "fairness," "liberty," "justice," "courage," "patriotism." It wasn't the words themselves, of course, but the system of values they represented. If conservatism means anything, it means a belief in and an attempt to adhere to a system of absolute values. But those politicians in whom conservatives had put their trust over the past decade had proved, for the most part, to be interested in those values only insofar as paying frequent lip service to them paid off in votes. Nor, with the exception of a few devout conservative spokesmen like William Buckley, did there seem to be any great interest in discussing the larger context in which the various fashionable issues of the day were set. The conservative "movement," especially in Washington, had grown increasingly "issue-oriented" and narrowly ideological. God often seemed to have been replaced by economics, which operated in the world through a mysterious force called "the market," thereby transforming much of contemporary conservatism into a flip-side version of dialectical materialism.

But then along came Carter, the only candidate in sight talking about absolute values, and he blind-sided the conservatives, cutting the high ground that they tended to think of as a birthright from under them, and in the process carrying along with him many of those working-class and middle-class Democrats who had defected from their party in 1972 and who were to form the electoral basis for the New Majority beloved by conservative theoreticians. Later, in the general election, many of them would vote for Ford. But although these Democrats have always been instinctively conservative, their votes had little or nothing to do with ideology. Instead, the vote for Ford was a vote for the familiar and a vote against such variables as a southern accent and a denominational affiliation, Southern Baptist, which still seems somewhat exotic and primitive in much of the country. It wasn't that Ford almost won the election; rather, Carter almost lost it, but that near-loss had little to do with what some conservatives found so appealing in early 1976. Part of it was owing to those factors over which he had no control, his accent among them. But much more of it was due to his apparent decision finally to bend to the dictates of the conventional wisdom and begin to address widely perceived "issues" in approved terms. He was no better at this than any other articulate politician echoing the established responses. His great appeal was that of the devout man speaking of the values that should be shaping our national life, and when he tried to assume the role of the professional politician addressing the trite and secondary "issues" of the day, he ended by losing many of us who thought of ourselves as crossover social conservatives.

Of course there weren't that many of us to begin with, and after a brief flirtation, he would probably have lost us anyhow, for what we like to identify as "conservatism," despite the sometimes intense efforts of its spokesmen to escape, still remains wedded to Republicanism, and there is still no divorce in sight. Whenever great social unrest stirs, as it did in the sixties, then there tend to be temporary alliances between conservatives and their roots in the Republican party and the social conservatives who form the backbone of the Democratic party. But when there is no longer a commonly perceived enemy—domestic Communists in the fifties, the New Left in the sixties—then they quickly demobilize and part company, much as soldiers do upon discharge.

There have been and continue to be many ingenious formulations devised for cementing this sometime alliance into something permanent. But in the end, two specters—one FDR, the other Herbert Hoover—seem to flit across the consciousness, and it's back to donkeys and elephants again. And no matter how you position them, the donkey and the elephant just can't mate.

After each such attempt, of course, some of us who cross over inevitably end up being stranded on the other side. And thus it was for many of us in 1976. Our instincts told us it should be Carter. But loyalty to recent experience required that it be either Ford or Reagan.

For those of us who had become radicalized—or counter-radicalized—in the sixties, Reagan exerted a powerful appeal. During my days at Berkeley, he had at times seemed the only visible and effective counterforce, the ony politician in the state and perhaps in the nation to stand against the fashionable barbarisms of the day. And not just a few of us felt this way. In 1966, in a 2 to 1 Democratic state, he won the gubernatorial election by a landslide, and it was, inevitably, against that backdrop of violent unrest and chaos, with scenes from Berkeley and characters from the New Left, that we best remember him.

It was this vividly remembered backdrop, however, that also raised certain inescapable questions. Could the Right, as we had come to know it over the decade that roughly corresponded to the period of Reagan's active political career, make its points without a radical Left to score against? Was Reagan perhaps the right man caught in the wrong time, a throwback to a very recent but rapidly fading past? Like Wallace, his forte was attack. But whom would he be attacking in 1976? And if he were unable to attack, would he be ineffectual?

At first, it seemed so. I had joined the Reagan campaign in Florida as reporter, just after he'd lost the New Hampshire primary. The loss had been a crushing one, primarily because of the high expectations in the Reagan camp. Reagan's own staff, along with most of the national media, had predicted a victory. A poll taken a week before the voting had shown Reagan with an 8-point lead, and despite the large uncommitted vote, the Reagan high command was sufficiently confident to leave New Hampshire two days before the primary to campaign in Illinois. Meanwhile, on primary eve, the Ford camp was so sunk in despair that Stuart Spencer, Ford's professional political manager, went to the unprofessional and somewhat startling length of publicly blaming Ford's anticipated poor showing on a conspiracy between Richard Nixon and John Connally.

When the dust cleared the day after the voting, however, the Ford people couldn't quite believe their eyes. A post-New Hampshire political cartoon sums it up. A slightly dazed sheriff in white grins down uncertainly at a smoking six-shooter held unsteadily in both hands. Sprawled in the dust is a lean Reaganesque gunfighter in black, his two drawn guns beside him. Says the befuddled Fordish figure; "Well, I'll be darned."

By most political standards, Reagan's extremely narrow loss would have been considered a moral victory, as was Eugene McCarthy's loss when he polled 42 percent in New Hampshire to Lyndon Johnson's 48 in 1968. But because Reagan had outorganized and outcampaigned an ineffectual and disorganized Ford, and because most accepted indicators signaled a win, Ford was very much the underdog, and his victory therefore a genuine upset.

As a result, the whole Reagan game plan had been thrown

into doubt. Ford was unelected, presiding over a Nixonless Nixon administration that seemed to lack purpose, direction, or philosophical underpinning. But Ford also had the White House; the pork barrel; the vast resources of the executive branch to draw on for position papers, speeches, and campaign personnel; the power to make or change national policy instantly; and the endorsement and active support of nearly every important party leader and most prominent establishment Republicans.

Therefore, it was essential to strike quickly by taking Ford out in New Hampshire and then in Florida. These victories, it was believed, would have a snowball effect, pushing Reagan over the top in Illinois and encouraging regular conservative Republicans to defect from Ford in droves. Thus, if it worked, the Reaganites believed they'd have a clear field by April.

But it didn't work, and when I briefly joined the Reagan campaign in Florida as a reporter in early March, it was a Reagan I'd never seen—waffling, tentative, defensive. This was not totally his fault. He and his advisers had agreed that if he were to run well in the general election, he'd have to start early to defuse the predictable charge of right-wing extremism. Thus, he muted the conservative trumpet and strove to sound statesmanlike. And then there was the social security problem. A bright young conservative on the Reagan staff had, as bright young conservatives tend to do, developed some highly intelligent and highly abstract positions on issues. One set of positions involved transfer programs and suggested ways to straighten out the social security system. It was an ingenious proposal, as proposals by bright young conservatives usually are, and Reagan liked it very much, using it as the basis for a major pre-New Hampshire speech.

The problem, however, is that right-wing candidates with national aspirations must never suggest they intend to tinker with things like social security. They must never, in fact, even say the words. But Reagan used the words, and suddenly all his attempts to sound statesmanlike seemed to go up in smoke. Ford immediately accused Reagan of advocating a voluntary social security system and of intending to invest social security funds in the stock market.

This was not the Reagan proposal. It wasn't even close. But the damage had been done. One of Lyndon Johnson's favorite stories concerned a Texas congressman who told his press aide to spread the story that his opponent fornicated with pigs. Can we prove it? asked the aide. Of course not, said the congressman. But it's a hell of a charge to have to spend your time denying. And that's what happened to Reagan. In Florida, the land of the retiree, there were the inevitable questions at every rally about social security and the elaborate explanations, with each explanation adding yet another element to the original statement. And so, in Florida, Reagan, who had been running well ahead in the polls, found himself sitting on a slipping landslide. The defensiveness was destroying him, and his aides realized he'd have to go on the attack if he were to survive into the later western primaries. But the problem was, Attack what?

Meanwhile, Ford had suddenly stopped bumbling and fumbling and bumping his head and came roaring into Florida, having discovered just what use the incumbency could be put to. And put it to use he did. Within a few days he promised Orlando that it would host an International Chamber of Commerce convention, offered Bay Pines a new veterans' hospital, tapped an extremely popular Florida conservative for a cushy post in the Treasury Deparment, promised Miami a whole new mass transit system, and then, with the large Dade County Latin audience much in mind, branded Fidel Castro, with whom Henry Kissinger had been playing footsie, "an international outlaw." And then, for good measure, he committed verbicide on one of the most hallowed terms of the Nixon-Ford-Kissinger administration: "I don't use the word détente anymore," he said solemnly.

"We've got the momentum," shouted an exuberant Ford in Florida, "and we're going to move and move and move." And for a time, move he did. He took Florida and then Illinois by ever-widening margins, and the presidential steamroller seemed to be picking up speed, carrying Ford toward Kansas City and a first-ballot nomination by acclamation, and leaving Ronald Reagan's political corpse flattened along the campaign trail somewhere between Illinois and North Carolina.

North Carolina was to be where the knockout punch would be delivered. During the week I traveled with Carter, our stay in a Winston-Salem hotel briefly overlapped with a stay by the Reagan entourage. The mood among the Reaganites was extremely low, and one of them told me it was all over. He and several others, apparently, were already negotiating for new jobs, and the word had spread that after he lost the primary, Reagan would withdraw.

The polls showed Ford running ahead, and North Carolina reporters assured me the polls were right. It was a power struggle, they pointed out, between Governor James Holshauser and Senator Jesse Helms. Holshauser, a moderately conservative Republican, had reportedly been promised a high post in the second Ford administration and was solidly in Ford's corner. (Had Ford been forced to deliver on all those promises, the national debt might have doubled and the size of the bureaucracy tripled.) Senator Jesse Helms, called by one reporter "the spokesman for the Fred Flintstone wing" of the Republican party, was Reagan's most fervent supporter, one of the very few in the Senate, and one of the very few politicians left who believed Reagan still had a chance. But that chance, he believed, depended entirely on Reagan reverting to the form that had electrified crowds during the Goldwater campaign and had carried Reagan to the governor's mansion in Sacramento in 1966.

Few of the political experts in North Carolina or in the nation agreed with Helms. The Ford-Holshauser versus Reagan-Helms confrontation was a microcosm of the civil war raging within the Republican party nationally, and the trend was obviously toward the moderate Republicanism represented by Ford. The Reagan Right, which had flourished in the sixties, was apparently dead, the experts believed—a belief shared by much of the Reagan staff, including John Sears, Reagan's campaign manager, who was later to come under heavy fire from conservatives for the Schweiker selection.

Sears had built the early phase of the Reagan campaign on several basic premises, among them that there was a strong anti-Washington mood in the country and that the campaign of 1976 would be a campaign of images and personalities rather than issues. This, however, proved to be both right and wrong. Thee was no doubt about the anti-Washington mood. But the idea of Reagan playing image politics was an extremely dubious one. It did seem to be working for Carter. But Carter wasn't playing old-fashioned image politics, à la John Kennedy or John Lindsay. No one talked about his movie-star good looks, nor were millions of American women yearning to run barefoot through his hair. Nor was it personality. People instead were searching for personal integrity and character. Politicians may confuse the two, but personality and character can be very different things.

And even if they were identical, the campaign strategy, while fine for Carter, was not right for Reagan. Reagan's special constituency, ideologically conservative Republicans, is perhaps the single most issue-oriented constituency in the country, and they had been dismayed by Reagan's performances in New Hampshire, Florida, and Illinois. Nor were things any better in North Carolina. Reagan was still trying to be statesmanlike, still trying to avoid anything that could be construed as a personal attack on Gerald Ford. The image may have been presidential, the stance statesmanlike. But that image and that stance, while perhaps potentially effective in the general election, was doing nothing to help Reagan in the primaries and a great deal to hurt him. Many of his supporters feared that perhaps age had finally overtaken him. They remembered the old Reagan and began to suspect that this new Reagan had insufficient fire in the belly. Nor was there much in this new approach to attract those who weren't quite sure about Ford. Ford, after all, was a decent man, no matter what words were put into his mouth. He also seemed sufficiently conservative to nonzealots, and he already had the job. Therefore, why turn him out? This was the question that Reagan's soft-sell image campaign couldn't answer.

Thus, North Carolina seemed to spell the end. But Senator Helms didn't think so. Against the advice of the Reagan national staff, he persuaded Reagan to buy statewide television time to show the film of a stem-winding speech in which Reagan, among other things, tore into détente with all the sharpness and fervor his supporters remembered from the sixties. That speech turned it around, and Reagan's victory in North Carolina was even more of a stunner than Ford's upset in New Hampshire.

From then on, the gloves were off. The money began to pour in again and Reagan swept through Texas, Indiana, and Nebraska, with the rest of the big western primaries just ahead. Part of his success was caused by the bungling of Ford and his advisers, whose inability to understand what was happening out in the country seemed to underscore the validity of the campaign charge that the Washington establishment was totally out of touch with the nation. Ford lost Texas, for instance, in large part because he signed an energy bill that Texans adamantly opposed; he appeared to believe they had supported it. And in his own state, Michigan, there was little serious thought given to a major effort until a new campaign staffer, James DeFrancis, administrative assistant to Senator Robert Griffin, pointed out to the Ford people that the primary in Michigan allowed crossovers, and there was a whole pack of former Wallaceites ready to crossover for Reagan. In the end, Ford won his own state's primary handily. But he might not have done so, had not an outsider shaken his campaign staff. And a loss in Michigan would have been the end.

In North Carolina, Reagan had proved that the Republican party was a least halfway hard-right, and from that moment on his primary campaign became an issue campaign. He still refused to attack Ford by name. But in his attacks on SALT, détente, deficit spending, and the Panama Canal, he was attacking our national leadership. And that meant, of course, he was attacking the Ford administration—and in the process, as it turned out, doing much of the preliminary campaigning for the Democrats by helping to discredit the Administration whose record they'd soon be challenging.

As the primaries wore on, the bad feeling on both sides intensified, culminating in the California primary, which left everyone with a bad taste. In June, Reagan and Ford were running neck and neck, both within grabbing distance of the nomination. Reagan was back in the West, home base, and he stumped California, delivering fire-eating versions of The Speech, hitting hard on such issues as SALT and détente and deficit spending. But it was with the Panama Canal issue that Reagan had found what reporters called his "Golden Kazoo," an emotional issue that transcends logical analysis, turning sedate, rational audiences into shouting, purse-waving mobs.

No one at the beginning of the campaign had predicted that the Panama Canal would become anyone's Golden Kazoo. In fact, in Florida, when Reagan first began mentioning it, the intense crowd response so startled him that he twice referred to it as the Canama Panal.

This is not to say that there aren't good reasons for the intensity of the reaction of the Canal issue. In the Northeast, it seems one of those abstract issues, like offshore drilling, for instance, which don't really touch our daily lives. And since what will and won't be political issues are primarily decided by networks and newspapers headquartered in the Northeast, it is understandable that no one hit on the Panama Canal as a key issue in early 1976. But people who live along such areas as the Gulf Coast see it very differently. The great port cities of the South and Southwest do a booming business as the result of Canal traffic, and the people in such parts of the country have a firsthand feeling for what the Canal means economically.

But that, of course, doesn't explain it all. Reagan played that Kazoo so effectively—and continues to play it today—because, like Carter, he seemed to understand the fundamental fact of the election year of 1976. As Carter put it, "something precious has slipped through our hands." Carter intended to refer in such statements to something a bit less tangible and much more profound than a canal, but the emotional thrust was essentially the same. Both Reagan and Carter spoke to what seemed to be a very real and very deep sense of loss, a clearly perceived breakdown of national will and national values.

Perhaps we were never quite the nation that we like to remember. But millions of voters believed we were, and Reagan and Carter, in very different ways, told them we could be that way again. If there had been a theme song for the 1976 primary campaign, it would have been "The Way We Were."

Ford, unlike Reagan, could never get a grip on that Kazoo and, in fact, seemed increasingly to lose his grip on his own campaign as the primaries dragged on. "There was," observed James Naughton of the *New York Times*, "something very basic lacking in the Ford campaign: "The fundamental flaw in the Ford campaign, as one of its operatives mused the other day, is that it never had a theme. It never had focus. 'We finessed it for a while,' he said, 'but we never got out front on the issues.' " Concludes Naughton: "It is not so surprising. The Ford campaign is a reflection of the Ford Presidency."

Like the Ford presidency, the Ford primary campaign had seemed to flip-flop from week to week. At times Ford attempted to present himself as "presidential," as if this were a quality that, like Ingredient X, could be arbitrarily added to the product. At other times, no doubt at the urging of the public-relations media types who dominated the Ford campaign, he seemed to be attempting to sell himself as if he were a cake of deodorant soap. At times, apparently acting on the advice of former Reagan adviser and political hardballer Stuart Spencer, he would launch personal attacks against Reagan, accusing him of irresponsibility, warmongering, and extremism in general.

Each of the approaches was tried in various primaries. But in California, during the last week of the primary campaign, all three came together. The week before, Ford had campaigned through the state, drawing small indifferent crowds, much less impressive than the crowds Reagan was drawing. The contrast was damaging, dramatized as it was on the daily network news, and so the decision was made to keep Ford out of the state during the last week and instead to flood California with televised political ads.

First came the ads showing Ford looking "presidential." Then came the "slice-of-life" commercials, in which actors and actresses dressed up like hardhats and housewives discussed in awed tones the things Ford had done for them.

"Notice anything about these fruit prices lately?" asked an actress-housewife.

"Well," answered her friend, "they don't seem to be going up the way they used to."

"President Ford has cut inflation in half," intoned the first housewife.

"In *half?*" gasped the second. "Wow!"

Wow, indeed. But at least the Ford campaign finally managed to get a laugh out of an audience, albeit for the wrong reasons. The laughter stopped rather abruptly, however, when the decision was made to attack Reagan directly in his own state. The occasion for the attack was a press conference at which Reagan, in response to a question about averting civil war in Rhodesia, rambled on vaguely, his statements sufficiently vague to allow the *San Francisco Chronicle* of June 3 to run the following headline: "Reagan Would Send GI's to Avert Rhodesia War."

The story was quickly picked up by the Ford camp, which put together a TV ad that ended with these words: "When you vote Tuesday, remember: Governor Reagan couldn't start a war. President Reagan could."

Now there is no doubt that Reagan's willingness to hypothesize about Rhodesia before newsmen was a blunder, much the same sort of blunder made early in the campaign when he rambled on about social security. And he did speak of sending American troops if the Rhodesian government requested them. But he spoke of those troops as part of a UN peacekeeping force, hardly a novel or extremist idea. Nor did he ever mention, as the Ford ad claimed, sending advisers or technicians, à la Vietnam.

Thus, the consensus among Reagan backers and many newsmen was that the Ford ad was the dirtiest bit of political pool since the 1964 LBJ ad that had Goldwater blowing a flower-picking little blonde girl to smithereens. But there was one great difference: Reagan and Ford belonged to the same political party.

Why Ford approved that ad has never been satisfactorily explained. It was, as everyone knew, totally unnecessary, since Ford had no chance at more than 40 percent of the California primary vote, and no last-minute effort could possibly have increased his total. Yet the attack was made, and made with relish, and its primary result was to add to the acrimony that divided—and continues to divide—a badly fractured party.

Ford supporters, attempting to justify it, maintained they were responding in kind. Reagan, after all, had been accusing the Administration of making massive concessions to our adversaries in Russia, Cuba, and Panama. But, responded the Reaganites, those attacks were aimed at policies rather than aspects of Ford's character.

Both sides had a point, and the whole argument would seem academic now, except for two basic points: it is indicative of a deep rift within the Republican party that shows no sign of healing; and something along the same lines promises to flare up again in 1980, when the two feuding wings of the GOP will once again have a go at each other. And as unlikely as it may seem, the cast of characters may be precisely the same. Ronald Reagan has let it be known that he is thinking seriously about running again, and Gerald Ford has let it be known that he will also run if necessary to stop Reagan.

The Ford-Reagan struggle—and especially the bitterness and rancor that characterized it—must puzzle many nonconservatives, to whom, no doubt, Gerald Ford and Ronald Reagan seemed about equally conservative in deed, if not always in word. Further, by 1976 the Republican party itself must have seemed monolithically conservative to most outsiders. Nelson Rockefeller, once the powerful leader of the party's influential liberal wing, had been dumped unceremoniously and almost contemptuously from the Ford ticket. Jacob Javits, once the scourge of contemporary conservatism, was viewed as an ineffectual and eccentric old uncle. Neither Senators Percy nor Brooks were taken seriously, and some liberals like Mathias of Maryland were talking—and continue to talk—about switching parties. It had, in short, become a conservative party with two apparently conservative candidates vying for the nomination. Therefore, why all the fuss and divisiveness?

Perhaps it's not possible to understand that without knowing something about conservative factionalism. There are, first of all, two basic groups of conservatives within the Republican party that, for lack of an adequately developed taxonomy, we might artificially designate as Republican-Conservative and Conservative-Republican. The first group, which includes Ford and which supported him in 1976, is composed of the great majority of congressional Republicans, the heirs of Robert Taft and midwestern Republicanism in general, that portion of big business that remains Republican, members of the Republican National Committee, once and future cabinet members, and the Republican estalishment in general.

The second group, the Conservative-Republicans (the hyphen is important) is in large part a grass-roots movement, thriving in those parts of the country we like to call the Sunbelt. These are the people who expect their Republicanism, like their biblical interpretation, to be served up fundamentalistically. And, to a great extent, they expect it to be served up by the intellectuals on the right, a small but highly articulate conservative group of writers and talkers. (Interestingly, there are no intellectuals left in the Republican center, and on the Republican left the Ripon Society, which once produced intellectuals in abundance, is now all but officially dead.)

Thus, if we want to strain the analogies to the snapping point and work in some class-struggle terminology, we might view it all, albeit somewhat fancifully, as a struggle between the proletarians and intellectuals on the one side, and the *bourgeoisie* of the Republican party on the other. (The aristocracy might have been represented at one time by the liberal Rockefeller wing.)

The bourgeois wing provides the basic strength and whatever stability the party has; the proletarian-intellectual alliance provides the ideology. But the bourgeois wing is usually reluctant to accept it, feeling that the parameters of ideology are usually set too narrowly and rigidly by the ideologists. The bourgeois wing believes itself to be conservative, and to outsiders it is. But conservative principles—or what have been defined as conservative principles—are secondary to Republican pragmatic principles. Thus, a Republican-Conservative will not hesitate to make a move unpopular with Conservative-Republicans—the China trip, SALT, economic controls—if he believes it necessary to the political success of the party.

These Republican-Conservatives inevitably see something potentially destructive in the activities of Conservative-Republicans, who they believe would rather go down in flames and take the party with them than compromise on an ideological principle. And they have a point. The majority of the Conservative-Republicans of the Washington variety—the intellectuals—believe they owe allegiance to the Republican party only insofar as it provides them with a satisfactory conservative political vehicle. Beyond that, they couldn't care less, and over the past half-decade the talk has increasingly turned to bolting the party. But the problem is that there's no place for them to bolt to. The Wallacites proved in 1976 they didn't want them. Nor are they of any use to the Democrats. So, at least for the time being, these Conservative-Republicans, as Richard Nixon used to set their teeth on edge by saying, have no place to go.

And even if there were some bolt-hole open to them, they might not be allowed to hurry toward it. The problem for the Conservative-Republicans during the Nixon years was that Nixon held their grass-roots, rank-and-file constituents on a short leash, so that whenever they stepped off to start a new movement, no one followed. And so inevitably, with great grumbling, they returned to the reservation.

With Nixon's departure, however, all that seemed to change and in 1975 and 1976 they were off the reservation in greater numbers than ever before, howling off down the warpath, but in a dozen disparate directions. There was the attempt to establish a third party by building on the foundation laid down by George Wallace. There were flirtations with fourth and fifth parties and ideas for new coalitions built around people like John Connally, who many conservatives persist in believing, against all evidence to the contrary, has a hold on a national constituency.

But in the end, especially with the total collapse of Wallace as a figure to be taken seriously, they returned to the reservation to do the yeoman work that almost resulted in Reagan's unprecedented nomination. This time, however, they are locked onto the reservation even more securely than they were held by Nixon, for the man who has become the single most powerful leader of grass-roots Republicans is Ronald Reagan, and Reagan is both a Conservative-Republican and a Republican Conservative. Thus, for as long as Reagan speaks for rank-and-file conservatives, which will probably be for as long as he wants to, then what Washingtonians like to call "the conservative movement" will remain largely locked into the Republican party, at least insofar as presidential politics are concerned.

Having said all this, however, it's necessary to take note here of a further fracturing of the "conservative movement" that could eventually have an effect on presidential politics. (I place the phrase "conservative movement" within quotation marks because it bothers me, since the essence of conservatism is not to move at all, but to sit there and prevent other things from moving. But I suppose it helps the image, just as it helped the image last year when the coach of the University of Oregon basketball team changed its name from "Ducks" to "Kamikaze Kids." Nevertheless, if it looks, quacks, etc.)

Within the "movement" itself, which excludes Birchers, Liberty Lobbyists, Nazis, and flat-earthers, there have long been two basic factions, lying along the New York-Washington axis. At the New York end is William Buckley and the group that clusters loosely around his *National Review*; at the Washington end are *Human Events*, a small handful of congressmen, and the American Conservative Union. Up until very recently, the Washington end of the axis, which might be called Low Church, continually chided the New York end, the High Church group, for being overly concerned with irrelevancies like literature and culture and values and God and not sufficiently militant on gut issues and the mechanics of Congress and getting good old Sonny Buggs elected to the House. It was the despair of the Low Church group that William Buckley, the unofficial High Church Pope, persisted in saying things like this: "Politics, it has been said, is the preoccupation of the quarter-educated, and I do most solidly endorse that observation, and therefore curse this century above all things for its having given sentient beings very little alternative than to occupy themselves with politics."

That sort of thing used to bedevil the Washington end of "the movement." Lately, however, they've had other things to worry about, chief among them the rapid growth of a new cluster of conservative organizations, grouped around the fund-raising operations of Richard Viguerie in Virginia. These groups view the *Human Events*–American Conservative Union as ineffective and lacking in political know-how, in much the same way that the *Human Events*–ACU people used to view *National Review*.

The effectiveness of these new groups in the areas of fund raising is unquestioned: Viguerie's direct-mail operation and his famous lists are already legendary in Washington. Their political effectiveness is another matter, however. For years now, one of the big "movement" problems in Washington has been its inability to get a significant number of right-thinking conservatives elected to Congress. Each year, to demonstrate their political prowess, they trot out an embarrassingly small group of representatives who were elected with "movement" help. But it remains a tiny group, and each year it's the same old bunch.

However, the new "movement" groups, who like to refer to themselves as the New Right, believe they're going to change all that, and have budgeted millions of dollars for carefully selected races in 1978. If they succeed in helping a significant number of conservatives to win races that they wouldn't have won ordinarily, then the New Right groups will become the new conservative power brokers in Washington, and their influence on presidential politics will be extremely significant. If they fail, then they will simply become another cluster in the great parade of political fund-raising groups that marches through Washington.

And, at any rate, for the time being, the New Right faces the same presidential problem as the Older Right (or perhaps the Middle-aged Right), and his name is still Ronald Reagan. Says Richard Viguerie: "The number-one problem of conservatism is that we've had a lack of leadership on the organizational level. Instead we've mistakenly looked to the man—like Goldwater or Reagan—who could call an audience to its feet.

That's not leadership. There's a big gap between Goldwater and Reagan and the next generation."

That may well be case. And there is little doubt that the New Right, which has already savaged Goldwater in its publications, would now like to see Reagan move on. He holds the key to grass-roots control, but in their eyes he is too much a man of the Old Right, too old and insufficiently populist for the New Right, which has a strong tendency toward and respect for Wallacism. Nevertheless, no matter how they talk about Reagan in private, in public they still have to pay him proper lip service. Because of his continued claim on the support of grass-roots conservatives, he exercises a significant amount of control over the future of their organizations.

And then, just to complicate matters further, there's the whole business of the *New* New Right. Poll after poll shows that the American people are increasingly disposed to call themselves conservative, and this trend is used by all segments of the Right to buttress their various positions and their claims to leadership. But this New New Right seems to have come from another direction entirely, and there is no reason whatsoever to believe they would look for leadership to the Old Old Right, the Old Right, the Middle-aged Right, or the New Right, for all these configurations, despite the breakaway attempts and ecumenical sentiments expressed by their leaders, remain rooted in the Conservative-Republican tradition, while this New New Right, which it has become fashionable to celebrate in places like *Newsweek*, comes out of another tradition altogether, and tends to find its leaders not among the Reagans but among the Gary Harts and Jerry Browns.

That, however, is the subject for another chapter, and has little relevance in any discussion of the immediate fate of the GOP. In 1980, as in 1976, the battle will once again be between the Conservative-Republican and Republican-Conservative wings of the party. Outsiders tend to believe that this time round it's wide open. But that is probably not the case. In all likelihood, unless things change drastically over the next two years, it will once again be Reagan against Ford, or failing that, a candidate with the blessings of the Reagan wing versus a candidate carrying the Ford seal of approval. The problem is that unless they're hiding behind something out there, no Republicans come to mind who fit either bill.

Non-Republicans don't quite see the problem. Many of them, for instance, see in Senator Howard Baker the perfect compromise candidate, with a foot in each camp. And many non-Washington Republicans no doubt share this view. Given what he has had to work with, he has done a good job as minority leader; he is personable and articulate; he has developed a national reputation for personal integrity; and he is neither ultraconservative nor ultraliberal.

Nevertheless, from the Washington perspective, his prospects are limited. The Republican-Conservatives grumble about his being pushy and opportunistic. The Conservative-Republicans grumble about what they call his vacillation, as when, for instance, he seemed to straddle both banks of the Panama Canal while the conservative Canal truth squads were stumping the country, cashing in on Reagan's Golden Kazoo.

In some ways this seems a puzzling reaction. There are very few men in Washington, after all, who are not pushy and opportunistic. If they lacked these qualities, most of them would still be back in Gobbler's Knob, practicing law. Nor are any of them beyond a little straddling when it promises to pay off politically. Even Conservative-Republicans aren't above sitting on their principles from time to time, as witness the ardent apologies for the selection of Richard Schweiker as Reagan's running mate in 1976. No, there's something more involved here, and one suspects it may be the Nixon factor.

The relationship between Nixon and Republicans in general and Conservative-Republicans in particular has never been a rational one. The first Washington political figure of note to call for his resignation was Senator James Buckley, one of the most respected of conservative spokesmen. But the people most loyal to Nixon during the last days tended, for the most part, also to be conservatives. Nor were Republican-Conservatives any less stout in their defense. The man who became spokesman for that wing, Gerald Ford, was smiting Nixon's enemies nearly to the last and, despite widely circulated reports to the contrary, was often doing so on his own initiative, and with relish. Further, in a very real sense, the Ford wing of the party finally was able to assert itself in presidential politics thanks to Nixon, whose creation President Ford was.

Republicans do not, of course, include Nixon's name when they call the roll of the party's greats. And no doubt they would flee screaming for the exits, were Nixon to appear at the next national convention. Nevertheless, the feelings about Nixon remain ambivalent, and despite the dislike many in both wings felt for him, the public posture that Republicans took toward him during Watergate seems to remain an unspoken and perhaps unconscious litmus test. And because of his starring role in the Watergate hearings, Baker cannot pass that test. But perhaps that is irrelevant, for neither wing of the party seems too interested in compromising this time around. Thus, Baker, who doesn't quite belong to either, will have a tought fight indeed for the nomination.

Nor, because the nominating process will most likely be in the hands of conservatives, do any of the new-look Republicans from out beyond the Potomac have high prospects in 1980. The most attractive of these is Governor Jim Thompson of Illinois. But he has already infuriated conservatives with his stands on abortion and the Equal Rights Amendment, and at this point it seems unlikely that anyone who infuriates conservatives will be nominated in 1980. Further, Thompson seems intent on soliciting support from what is left of the Rockefeller aristocratic-liberal wing of the party, and that is one of the quickest routes to the Republican guillotine. After 1980, which may represent the final dance of the old elephants, there will no doubt be a free-for-all for control of the party, much as there was among Democrats in 1976. At that time the Thompsons and the Danforths and all those others beyond the pale will have a chance. But this time round, the Conservative-Republicans and Republican-Conservatives who decided things in 1976 will probably decide things in 1980. Thus, the nominating process may effectively lock out any young Lochinvar.

No doubt these pronouncements all seem somewhat dogmatic, and it is admittedly foolhardy to make long-range political predictions. All sorts of things could happen between now and 1980. Reagan could suddenly begin to run, like the portrait of Dorian Gray. Or Ford could suddenly see the light and go off traveling to spread the Good News with Bill Bright's Campus Crusade for Christ International.

But barring unforseen events—that Second Coming for which Jimmy Carter is preparing, for instance—chances are good that it will be Reagan against Ford, one more time. Ford has told friends he doesn't want to run again. But he has also said he will do so if it is necessary to stop Reagan. He could run one of his protégés like Donald Rumsfeld as a proxy candidate. But most of Ford's protégés, all of whom have strong congressional ties, are not acceptable out in the grass roots. And that leaves Ford himself.

Reagan has not said publicly that he will run. But there is good reason to believe that he has told his 1976 campaign high command to begin gearing up for the 1980 race. Nor will he rule out a run when questioned by reporters; thus, despite the absence of a firm commitment, his grass-roots supporters are held in place. Reagan might also be holding them for a protégé, of course. But the problem is that he doesn't seem to have one. There are several effective Conservative-Republican spokesmen in the Senate, and a few more than that in the House. But with the exception of representative Philip Crane of Illinois, none of them are at this writing up to a presidential race. Thus, Reagan seems almost inevitable, and his grass-roots and intellectual supporters believe he can have the 1980 nomination for the asking.

It won't be easy, of course. Nothing in politics is ever there for the asking. But the Reagan forces will be much more in control of the grass-roots organizations this time round, and the Conservative-Republicans are much more effective than the Republican-Conservatives at mobilizing the troops for the primaries. They know now, in hindsight, that had the strategy for the first few primaries in 1976 been different, and had they been more diligent in rounding up the delegates, Reagan could have had the nomination with relative ease. And the next time, they are convinced, they will have the delegates.

Republican-Conservatives, of course, dispute this. Despite minimal Reaganite inroads, they still effectively control the official party apparatus, and given another Ford-Reagan shoot-out, nearly every Republican of note, past and present, will once again back Ford. Their arguments the next time around will be similar to the most basic arguments of 1976, chief among them the argument of electability. Only Ford, his supporters argued, had a chance against a unified Democratic challenge in 1976. Reagan might have exerted strong appeal among the true believers and intense single-issue groups on the right, the argument ran. But averaged out among the population as a whole, the Golden Kazoo ignites very few indeed. Perhaps. But the argument was greatly defused by Ford's loss, proving in the most elementary way that he wasn't electable after all. Further, the Reaganites argue, Reagan is manifestly the superior campaigner, superb on the attack. And it would take an intelligent and sustained attack to unhorse Carter.

These and other old arguments will probably be rehearsed once again in 1980, and perhaps some basic questions will be answered. Perhaps we will find out whether what remains of the Republican party is hard Right, as the Reaganites claim, and whether the power of the Republican-Conservative wing is merely paper power, a vestigial construct with its visible leadership totally out of touch with the Conservative-Republican rank and file and the new conservative currents that are flowing through the nation. Or perhaps we'll find out that the old Republican-Conservative wing is in fact sufficiently conservative for the nation's taste and that what is needed, as we are frequently told, is to build upon that wing in an effort to broaden the party's base.

These are just a few of the possibilities. But there is another: 1980 may represent the last battle of the old elephants as we have come to know them, just as 1976 represented the final appearance on the national scene of so many of the old Democratic donkeys who had shaped our society over the past several decades. And once the old elephants have been laid to rest in the boneyards, we may find something totally unpredicted dancing on their graves.

We seem to be coming to the end of one distinct period, during which most of us cut our political and ideological teeth. And now there seems to be something as yet shapeless stirring around out there, something that defies political labeling and shuns all the old ideological tags. There are new people out there, many of them looking and sounding a great deal like Jerry Brown, smiling strangely at the establishment categorizers and classifiers, their heads popping up all over the political landscape like asparagus shoots in springtime.

Conservative? Moderate? Liberal? Perhaps all of these. Perhaps one or two of them. Or perhaps none of them at all. Perhaps, in places like California, people like Jerry Brown are working on a whole new dictionary of American politics.

CHAPTER ELEVEN

A few months ago, on my last trip to California, I changed planes at O'Hare Airport in Chicago. On the first leg of the trip, I read an issue of *Newsweek*, which told me, among other things, that Jerry Brown and Gary Hart were among the nation's most important conservative spokesmen. Conservative. Puzzling. Reagan? No mention at all.

At O'Hare, with an hour to wait, I walked through the terminal. Near the TWA ticket counter there was a commotion, apparently some sort of New Leftish demonstration. Kids were waving signs, handing out leaflets, and lecturing passersby. One of them stood out, a strikingly attractive girl holding up a large sign, upon which, in big letters, was printed the word "SEX." Businessmen were bumping into one another to get a better look, and when they stopped, the other demonstrators, or whatever they were, buttonholed them and sold them papers and magazines.

An intriguing sign. But as you came closer, you saw words in small black letters above the big red "SEX," spelling out this sentence: "Nuclear power is even better than SEX." Aha, you thought. They're *conservative* kids. But not at all. It was the U. S. Labor party, battling the "forces of no-growth" and the "antiscience mob" in Washington who want to slow down nuclear development.

Then there was the race that wasn't, potentially the most fascinating match up of them all: S. I. Hayakawa versus Tom Hayden for the Senate. Hayakawa, like Reagan, was a conservative icon from the sixties who had made a national reputation by battling the disciples of Tom Hayden at San Francisco State. Hayakawa himself did not then nor does not now feel comfortable with the conservative label. He is, he insists, as do many academics of the *Commentary–Public Interest* stripe, an old-line liberal who stands now where he stood decades ago. But in the sixties the country lurched violently leftward, so that the spot on which he continues to stand now seems to lie distinctly toward the right.

But that, of course, is the story with many of us, and the old-line liberal of the fifties, simply by standing still in the California of the sixties, became the Reagan conservative of the seventies. Indeed, that is what happened to Ronald Reagan himself, who began as a Democrat. And if the violent movements of the sixties pulled the old liberal-left rightward, then by the mid-seventies they had also pulled the New Left of the sixties toward the Center, as witness the sudden respectability of Tom Hayden, founder of Students for a Democratic Society, member of the Chicago Seven, father of Berkeley's Red Tribe. Perhaps nothing better demonstrates how dramatically things have shifted over the last decade than the nearly successful candidacy of that man for the U. S. Senate. "The radicalism of the sixties is the common sense of the seventies," said Hayden frequently, and a significant number of nonradical Californians seemed to agree.

There was also the Reagan-Ford confrontation, and perhaps most fascinating of all, the nonconfrontation between Jimmy Carter and Jerry Brown, who almost casually entered four primaries in which Carter ran in 1976 and beat him in each of them. Unlike Ford in his race, Carter stepped carefully in California, content to challenge Church for second place, thus avoiding a potentially damaging showdown. Brown does not like Carter, and the feeling is mutual. Had Carter tried to carry the fight to him in his own state, as Ford did to Reagan, then the Ford-Reagan shoot-out would have seemed tame in comparison.

This deep and instinctive mutual loathing seems strange at first glance, for on the surface the two men appear much alike. Carter, the born-again Baptist, and Brown, the former Jesuit seminarian, both exert a strong moral and frequently semireligious appeal. Both rose to power in great measure on their own, with minimal help from the establishment that controlled their parties. Both understood and spoke to most of the basic causes of the malaise afflicting post-Vietnam, post-Watergate America. And both understood that a totally new language was necessary to address those concerns.

Yet despite the superficialities, the differences are profound. Neither accepts the convenient political pigeonholes we have developed for what we call "issues," and each seems to understand that "issues" are simply single symptoms of much larger matters. But there the similarities end. Carter, the born-again Protestant, sees the world from the inside out, with the emphasis on the individual conscience functioning within an immutable framework of religious and moral values and commandments. Brown, the former Jesuit who shared the sixties fascination with Zen, consciousness raising, and various forms of mysticism, seems more to see the world from the outside in, the semireligious tendencies that appear to inform both his rhetoric and his way of life being more properly cultural than traditionally religious. In this sense, those who charge that Brown is superficial have a point, but it may miss a larger one. If Carter is a moral President, then Brown may be a manners governor. But manners, the outward expression of a culture, or the way of life of a given society, while by definition superficial, may also be the surest guides to a society's soul. And the politician who masters the manners and understands firsthand the culture of his society may just hold the secular soul of that society in his hands.

This is not to suggest that Brown is a more formidable politician than Carter, or vice versa. That's something we may discover in 1980. But in 1976, at least, both seemed to have tapped something profound and basic, something not understood by other national politicians or by those who write and comment on politics. Nevertheless, while both of them tapped something deep and real, they may not have tapped the same thing at all. Carter, with his appeal to morality, could not strike the right sparks in California, nor can he do so today. Nor could Brown, with his essentially cultural appeal, strike the right sparks in Georgia, were he to try to do so.

Perhaps the basic differences between Georgia and California are instructive. Perhaps the instinctive distaste Brown and Carter feel for each other grows out of a tension as old as Western society. Matthew Arnold put it this way: "The governing idea of Hellenism is spirit of consciousness, that of Hebraism, strictness of conscience."

I don't intend here to try to add new terms to a political landscape already cluttered with labels and descriptive phrases. There are problems enough in trying to define something like "the new conservatism," for which we are just now being told that Jerry Brown is a spokesmen, without muddying things further by throwing "Hellenism" and "Hebraism" into the discussion in a way that would no doubt cause Arnold to writhe in his grave. Nevertheless, if we're to come to some conclusions about this phenomenon being somewhat loosely called "the new conservatism" or "the New New Right," we have to push some terms around and ask some simple questions. Is there something happening out there of sufficient import to prompt *Newsweek* to ask on its cover whether America is turning right? If so, how does it translate into politics? And who are the politicians who are tapping it? How do you get from Barry Goldwater to Nixon-Agnew to Ronald Reagan to Jimmy Carter to Jerry Brown and the politics of the eighties? And most important of all, who are these "New Rightists" or "New Conservatives," if in fact they exist at all?

Again, perhaps the best place to look is in the California of the 1976 elections, where nearly all the relevant political terms could be applied to various politicians and the groups whose votes they attempted to solicit.

First there were the old-line liberals, a once-powerful but now rapidly dying breed whose pedigree runs straight back to the New Deal. The most vibrant and articulate of the last of the New Deal politicians was Hubert Humphrey, whose death seemed symbolic of the end of three decades of political dominance. Already, however, in 1976, it was clear that the line had run out. When the year began, the smart money was riding on Humphrey. Halfway through the primary season, however, it was obvious that Humphrey no longer commanded the allegiance of a national constituency of sufficient size and vitality to win him—or anyone from his wing of the party—the nomination. Thus, in California in 1976, Church and Udall seemed to run almost ghostly campaigns, their support coming primarily from the old-line liberal Democratic faithful, many of them academics who still tend to take people like John Kenneth Galbraith and Norman Cousins very seriously and still believe the United Nations means something.

Interestingly enough, the extremes on both the Left and Right of California politics also seemed to have atrophied in 1976 in a state famous for its extremists. On the Right, the John Birch Society, which had run the California Wallace campaign in 1968, had few candidates and made little noticeable impact. Nor did the equivalent leftist groups such as the Peace and Freedom Party make any significant difference.

But while the old liberalism tottered along on its last legs, and while the extremes seemed to be in the process of dropping off, the old conservatism seemed alive and well in California in 1976, as witness the strong showing of Hayakawa and Reagan.

A caveat may be in order here, however, before we proceed with any discussion of the "old conservatism," for in California, traditional conservatism means Reagan conservatism, and Reagan conservatism exerts an appeal extending well beyond the rigid limits of right-wing ideology, which may explain why the John Birch Society tends to view Reagan as public enemy number one.

Nevertheless, despite the relatively broad appeal of Reagan conservatism, it is built on the bedrock "old conservative" constituency of economic conservatives, the same people who formed the backbone of the Goldwater movement and who still believe that something can be done about deficit spending, the debasement of the dollar, taxes, inflation, and the massive federal government that causes all these problems.

The second large block of "old conservatives" is actually relatively new, most of them being middle-class and blue-collar Democrats who began to vote Conservative-Republican shortly after the McGovernites took control of the Democratic party and the New Left moved off the campuses and into the streets. The social conservatives tend to retain their original party affiliation, and there are many Republicans they will not vote for. But given a choice between a conservative and a liberal, they almost always vote conservative, no matter what the party.

Then there is another group, this one having come to accept certain aspects of the old conservatism in the seventies because of genuine alarm over how close the government is circling in toward control of our personal lives. For some it is schools, for some the reverse discrimination implicit in such programs as affirmative action, and for some it may be something as simple as the threatened saccharin ban. Political scientists and analysts no doubt take such things lightly; but perhaps no recent governmental action has more dramatically brought home to ordinary, nonideological Americans how ubiquitous federal regulations have become than the FDA's attempt to confiscate their Fresca and Diet Pepsis. (This is not to say that all such people, alarmed at federal intrusiveness, automatically become Reagan conservatives. In California, many of them are also attracted to Jerry Brown, who views the federal government and the bureaucracy with great contempt.)

Finally, there are the single-issue enthusiasts, for whom Reagan plays the Golden Kazoo, as he did in 1976. There is a great deal of confusion about this group. The tendency among those analyzing "the new conservatism" is to classify them as the ideological shock troops of the New Right movement. But in fact, no one is quite certain who they are, where they come from, or what motivates them. They may be little more than flip-side radicals, reacting to current social trends. Thus, for every gay rights demonstration, there is sure to be a corresponding antihomosexual rally. For every pro-ERA group, there is an equally militant anti-ERA organization, and so on down the line.

But there is obviously something more than simple flip-side radicalism at work here. Although you may disagree with the whole business, or be indifferent to it, you can understand what compels a woman to get out and demonstrate for the Equal Rights Amendment. But it is much more difficult to understand the woman who gets out to demonstrate against it with almost fanatical intensity. If she is a woman whose home and family are her career, as seems to be the case with most ERA opponents, passage of ERA would have no effect on her life whatsoever.

Undoubtedly, many such demonstrators are marching to the tune of the Golden Kazoo, seeing in things like ERA a symbolic threat to a way of life that seems to be slipping away. And in areas such as antihomosexual activity, the motivation seems clearer, for many of us sincerely believe that homosexuality is a form of mental illness and that homosexuals routinely attempt to proselytize. Thus, it is perfectly understandable that mothers object to such things as having their children taught by homosexual teachers, even as many of them objected to them being taught by Marxist-oriented teachers in the fifties and sixties.

Nevertheless, such explanations don't quite do it. The pro-ERA, proabortion, prohomosexual rights, and progroups in general come out of the activist tradition of the militant Left, which, interestingly enough, increasingly enjoys the support of the federal government. But the antis, for the most part, were not long ago charter members of the group we called the Silent Majority. No doubt many of them became sensitized during the sixties by the demonstration-confrontation tactics of the Left, blown up to national proportions by the media, and have adopted the same tactics, realizing that a demonstration against anything in a major media center is certain to make the evening news.

But these are purely tactical considerations, and one suspects that the "why" lies a good deal deeper. There are any number of explanations, ranging from the social to the psychological. But perhaps the most plausible explanation centers in religion, for it is only when viewed from the religious perspective that the intensity of many of these single-issue demonstrators seems to make sense. The antiabortion forces, for instance, while not monolithically Roman Catholic, are nevertheless for the most part led by Catholics, for whom abortion is murder, and therefore the deadliest sin. The leaders of the antihomosexual movement are fundamentalist Christians, who believe the Bible's—and therefore God's—injunctions against sexual deviance couldn't be clearer. And among the ERA opponents are a significant number of Christians who believe that such an amendment would violate the divine plan for the structure of the family, and therefore the structure of society, which they believe God intended to be built upon the family.

Although many of these people have been born again, and although their activities may be yet one more manifestation of the national religious revival that helped carry Carter into office, few of them are Carter people. This is especially true in California and in much of the Southwest, where religious fundamentalism has long been identified with political conservatism. Among such people, Carter's social Christianity is deeply suspect. And in places like California, the land of the raised consciousness, they have seen quite enough of Hellenism and demand their Hebraism straight and undiluted. Thus, for the most part, the single-issue antis line up politically with Reagan conservatives. Reagan himself does not speak of a deep personal religious commitment. But he plays all the right tunes on all the right issues, and his positions can therefore be seen as divinely directed.

Thus, it seems just short of absurd to lump these single-issue conservatives and the Reaganite Right of both parties together with the supporters of Jerry Brown and file them all under the heading "the New Right" or "the new conservatism." There may indeed be something stirring that merits those labels. But the old conservatism remains the old conservatism, and Ronald Reagan remains its national political spokesman. If there is a new conservatism, and if its spokesman is Jerry Brown, then its roots are set in very different soil.

First of all, there is Brown himself, the first and most prominent of what promises to be a new generation of new-breed politicians. Brown is very different from the crop of politicians from which we have been accustomed to picking our national leaders over the past three decades. This basic difference isn't a matter of the mattress on the floor or the dirty old car or the alternate junk food and health food diets or the Zen or the Jesuitical casuistry or serving cold cuts and diet Ginger Ale to Prince Charles during his California visit. These things have endeared Brown to a national media with an increasingly insatiable appetite for anything new, and they are a very important part of his cultural appeal. But what distinguishes Brown from the ruck of conventional national politicians is where he comes from—or, for that matter, where he doesn't come from.

Alone among the contenders with serious or semiserious aspirations for the presidency in 1976, Brown's personal political roots did not extend back to the old New Deal, when the liberal and conservative positions as we have come to know them were first firmly established. For the most part, the other candidates came into maturity during the forties, when World War II, played out against the backdrop of the Great Depression, was the central experience.

Brown, however, came to manhood during the sixties, with Vietnam providing the central experience for a generation as yet only imperfectly understood by the veterans of the forties. Other presidential aspirants attempt to speak to that experience, and judged solely on the current political rhetoric, one would think there had never been any hawks in the Democratic party. But Brown is different. He doesn't need to strain to understand that experience. He lived it. "I started in politics by opposing the war in Vietnam," he says. "I don't think it was right, and I think it has seriously undermined the position of America in the world. It has weakened the social and political fabric of our country. And it is going to take heroic efforts to rebuild America because of it."

Brown's credentials as a member of the sixties generation are impeccable. While the other presidential hopefuls were either serving in Washington or plotting to get there, Brown was serving a tour at Berkeley. In the sixties, while Washington was the capital of establishment America, Berkeley was the national capital of the counterculture. True, his exposure to the activism there may have been superficial, as his critics charge. But he was there, and no others aspiring to be President can make that claim. Thus Brown, unique among national politicians with presidential aspirations, speaks to and for a whole new generation as yet untapped by any of his competitors.

There has as yet been surprisingly little written about the later lives of that generation of the sixties and early seventies, the largest and best-educated generation ever produced in America. For a decade we became accustomed to watching them demonstrate nightly on the evening news, and then one day the cameras focused elsewhere, and it was almost as if they'd just stepped off Jerry Brown's Spaceship Earth and disappeared. But they hadn't, of course. Like every other generation, they went off to get jobs, get married, buy homes, and have children. Like generations before them, they settled into what we still call the middle class. But there was a difference. This generation, unlike any other before it for the past three decades, had been radicalized. And the radicalism of the sixties, to paraphrase Tom Hayden, became the middle-class values of the seventies.

This is not to say that all the college students of the sixties were closet SDSers. The actual membership of the various New Left organizations was never large. But on campuses like Berkeley, the activists and nonactivists shared the same culture, and once the social mores of any culture have been accepted, the political attitudes are also extremely easy to accept. This is not a complicated process, requiring any great analysis. The key is peer pressure, and few of us have not felt it. In the sixties, when you arrived on campus, you'd be a very unusual individual indeed if you refused to listen to rock, smoke a joint, take advantage of the new attitudes toward sex, or wear your hair long. Nor would you be likely to dissent from the various prevailing political views. You might not actually take to the barricades. But your sympathies would be more likely to lie with those who did than with, say, your parents, who were probably going to vote for Reagan and Nixon.

There is little of ideology involved in all this, But the desire for the approbation of your peers may be a more powerful force in shaping basic attitudes and practices than all the ideologies yet devised.

And in the sixties, it was a powerful force indeed. Perhaps, because it is essentially a cultural phenomenon, behavior induced by peer pressure tends to be viewed as superficial and transitory. But in the sixties this was not the case. It may initially have been peer pressure and cultural conformity that dictated the shape of the political beliefs of those students who demonstrated in the streets of Chicago. But it was something a good deal more than superficial that drove them into those streets. The process may begin with something apparently superficial like peer pressure, but it obviously ends by sinking in very deeply. You don't stand your ground in city streets and allow yourself to be brutalized for something you wear lightly on the surface.

All of this was especially true at Berkeley, where the counterculture was the only culture. It affected everyone, and few people understood how deep it went until something like the People's Park riots erupted, next to Kent State the largest and bloodiest confrontation on any campus during the decade. There were a number of reasons for the People's Park riots, perhaps the two most basic being the ineptitude of the consistently inept university administration and the skill of the Berkeley activist leadership in manufacturing an issue. But the reasons are irrelevant. What is significant is that thousands of Berkeleyites took to the streets to march through tear gas, bullets, and the combined police forces of a significant portion of northern California in a demonstration so massive that the university asked Governor Reagan to send in the National Guard. Later, it was estimated that in one way or another, 15,000 students had been involved, among them fraternity and sorority members, athletes, cheerleaders—a cross section of the campus, including all those types we had become accustomed to calling "straight." The issue, whether to preserve a small grassy plot off Telegraph Avenue or to put a building on it, was basically a cultural issue. But the response was political, and it demonstrated beyond a doubt that at Berkeley—and on campuses and in university communities across the country much like it—the culture of the sixties provided a fertile breeding ground for a powerful new cultural politics.

The veterans of Chicago and People's Park have moved out into the nation now, and with them they have carried a set of cultural and political attitudes that were forged in the sixties and are very different from those to which we have grown accustomed, and the temptation among politicians who did not share or do not understand the sixties experience is to write them off as apolitical. They seem to vote in no predictable way; in fact, most of them don't seem to vote at all. But this may be a profound misreading of what could become a powerful new political force. True, they are apolitical in one basic sense—established parties, established ideologies, and established issues don't mean a fig to them. Nor will they vote for anyone who does not understand and speak to their concerns. When one of their own runs, however, they suddenly appear at the polls in force, as witness the startling showing of Tom Hayden, who had been expected to garner only a handful of votes in the 1976 primary.

It is this group, perhaps more than any other, that forms the basic Jerry Brown constituency. Brown also commands the allegiance of many Democratic regulars, of course, for the majority of loyalists in both parties will always ride with a winner. But it is this special new constituency that is uniquely Brown's own. He speaks their language, and he understands a central fact that has eluded other national politicians: among members of the sixties generation, culture and politics are inseparable. Cultural statements are political statements, and the most important political concerns are also cultural concerns.

Perhaps nothing is more indicative of Brown's political acuity than his ability to address the concerns of this group directly while at the same time striking responsive chords in older, very different, and more traditional groups. Consider this typical statement, for instance: "The federal government is taking onto itself more and more power for local matters for everything from family planning to criminal justice to health service. Clearly, national issues are not being addressed in a straightforward way while everyone on the other side of the Potomac starts meddling in local and state affairs because of the lack of faith in the ability of people to govern themselves. Decentralization of power—that is important to me. All those things that can be left at a lower level of political organization ought to be."

That is a statement that could just as well have been made by Ronald Reagan, and these anti-Washington sentiments, with which Brown tends to lace his public utterances, have earned him a small but significant cadre of old conservative followers. And such sentiments, albeit for very different reasons, also appeal strongly to his special sixties constituency, explaining, perhaps, why they are being lumped into the "new conservatism" category.

In both cases, Brown speaks directly to the distrust of the federal government that may be the most significant political development of the seventies. The Reagan conservatives have always distrusted it, although it can be argued that in the sixties this distrust seemed to become a bit selective, as when conservatives suddenly became champions of the big government in Washington that waged the war in Vietnam and cracked down on demonstrators protesting that war. Nevertheless, despite the flirtation with statism in the sixties, and despite its continued willingness to approve governmental intervention to put down what it tends to view as aberrant personal behavior, Reagan conservatism remains hostile to centralized national government, the basic critique being economic.

Brown's sixties generation also dislikes the government in Washington, although the sources of that dislike are very different. Again, as with the contradictory impulses that have left many Reaganites philosophically stranded somewhere between the opposing extremes of statism and libertarianism, so does much of the sixties generation often seem to be struggling to reconcile certain irreconcilable polarities, This was especially true of the New Left during its heyday. Its ultimate vision, albeit it a fuzzy and seldom articulated one, was of a socialist society. But the problem for the Left, whether old or new, is that the sixties left the rising generation with a total distrust of centralized government and a total contempt for the men who run it. The catch, however, is that you can't by definition have socialism without a strong central government.

Much of the liberal Left simply dodges the question, insisting that our problems were not caused by the government itself but by the men who ran it. The possibility that similar men will once again run it is simply ignored, and many liberals who feel this way were perfectly content with Jimmy Carter's brand of anti-Washingtonism. Carter never told us he would reduce the size of government or cut back on its activities; instead, he promised he would streamline it and make it more efficient — not a particularly heartening promise for those who fear the government's intrusiveness, as do a majority of Brown's sixties constituency. And perhaps, if we could put ourselves in their places, we'd find this fear perfectly understandable. Just as the men who went to Washington in the early sixties were the best and brightest, as David Halberstam has called them, so were the students who flooded our campuses during the first part of that decade the best and brightest generation yet produced in America, the flowering of several generations of the finest liberal education. They had been taught to use their minds; they had been taught to think for themselves; they had been taught to accept nothing at face value; they had been taught to be critical. And that, as things began to fall apart and the national mood soured, is precisely what they did. They heeded what their professors and their administrators did, rather than what they said, and discovered, as we all eventually discover, that hypocrisy is the glue that holds the social structure together. They turned their attention to their government and found it to be run by the same men who ran their universities and attempted to control their lives. There was a difference, however. The men who ran academia wanted them to fit quietly into grooves they had nothing to do with creating; but the men who ran the government wanted them, literally, to turn over their lives. They had been taught and encouraged to be critical and analytical. But when they applied that critical and analytical eye toward their universities and their government, and when they began to protest against what they found, they were told to desist. Do what you're told, they were ordered, and when they didn't their administrators and their government officials called in the police and then the troops. The administrators told them to stop protesting the war, and the government told them that their generation was expected to fight in it. But under the tutelage of their professors and then on their own, they had examined that war critically and analyzed it ad infinitum, and had found it absolutely wrong. As students, they believed it their right and duty to do so. And having done so, they found it morally repugnant that they and their generation were being ordered to cooperate in the commission of a moral evil.

Their analyses may have been faulty, and I believe that to an extent they were. But the question became whether they had the right to make them, and that is a question that should never have been asked. Nor should it have come as a shock that they responded in the way they did. It may or may not be a healthy practice to raise your children progressively and permissively. But once you have decided to do so, you cannot, somewhere around their seventeenth birthday, suddenly shout at them to straighten up, get hair cuts, and do as you say, not as you do.

The sixties generation was deeply scarred by the Vietnam experience, and it profoundly altered the way many of them in normal times would have come to view the role of the government. During a more placid period, the sixties college graduates would have left the campuses for the most part imbued with the liberal leftism preached by their professors, believing absolutely that all our social problems could be solved if the federal government set out to do so. The experience of the sixties made that view impossible.

The Vietnam experience resulted in creating what looks like a very similar attitude toward government between the Brown constituency and the Reagan conservatives. But it also defines the difference between them, and explains why they can never make common cause down the line. The Reagan

Right, and most of the country's conservatives, unquestioningly backed our involvement, and continue to do so. And they continue to be the most ardent champions of America's interventionist role in the world, our foreign policy and its conduct being perhaps the single greatest conservative litmus test today. It's extremely difficult, however, to imagine any of the sixties constituency making common cause with Reaganites on such matters as, say, the Panama Canal, or SALT, or the Pentagon's budget, or any of the other national-defense issues that send conservatives boiling into the streets. Like the Little Englanders, the sixties constituency has heard the great recessional, and given the events of the past decade, it is difficult to condemn their attitude. Odd, that we should be ending the era beginning with World War II with the most conservative of us, their roots in the America-First, isolationist tradition blowing the interventionist trumpet; while the generations with its roots in the liberal Left, where once the most rabid interventionists reigned, now call for America to come home to stay.

There are other basic differences between the Reagan Right and the Brown constituency that argue against any effective political alliance, especially in those areas of concern that we call the social issues. They do not, for instance, oppose such policies as busing, in part because of their conviction, heightened by the Vietnam experience, that ours is a racist society that owes a special duty to those it has exploited, and perhaps in part because as well-educated middle-class types they tend, unlike say a blue-collar social conservative living in a working-class neighborhood, to have the wherewithal to insulate themselves from the social disruption that accompanies such policies. Nor, on any of those social issues touching upon personal behavior and freedom, do the sixties constituency and the Reagan Right come close to standing on common ground. Again, a somewhat odd reversal. Conservatives, who above all like to think of themselves as champions of individual freedom, tend in practice—the marijuana decriminalization issue, for instance—to take the more repressive and statist position, while the group with its roots in the liberal Left, which frequently seems intent on regulating everything we inhale or ingest, takes the erstwhile conservative position in favor of maximizing personal freedom.

Nevertheless, although the differences run deep, growing as they do out of totally different traditions and experiences, many of the manifestations of social and political discontent take similar forms among both groups. Jerry Brown seems to understand this, and alone among national politicians he can speak to both groups and convince many members of each that he is speaking their language.

When Brown speaks of limits to growth, for instance, many traditional conservatives hear a call to limit the growth of government, while his sixties constituency hears a call for a sharp curtailment of industrial growth. When he calls for a limit to new programs spinning out of Washington traditional conservatives hear it as a call for fiscal responsibility, while the sixties constituency hears it as a call for those aliens who gave us Vietnam and then Watergate, which confirmed everything ever said about the government from the steps at Sproul Hall in Berkeley, to stay out of their lives.

Brown need not always say these things; the way he lives also makes a statement to each of these groups. The stripped-down, laid-back life-style is refreshing to Middle American social conservatives who had grown increasingly uneasy about such things as Richard Nixon's new operetta costumes for the White House police or Spiro Agnew's vacations with Frank Sinatra at Palm Springs or the legions of bright young White House aides with their door-to-door limousine service.

The sixties constituency sees it as an indication that his head is in the right place, and that he is one of them. In a sense, this may be the most self-centered generation in our history. There is a constant preoccupation with consciousness, with the body and what you put into it. Yet at the same time, there is an equally strong preoccupation with the need to simplify, to push back toward basics, to get the clutter out of one's life. These two tendencies may seem nearly antithetical to those of us who don't belong to the sixties generation. But they are there, and Jerry Brown seems to personify them, at least to the extent that they can be personified in political life.

Again, there seems to be something very basic involved here that perhaps just can't be understood by those of us who grew up in an earlier and much less prosperous period, as most of our national politicians did. Against the backdrop of the Great Depression, the drive among all good men was toward security and the acquisition of sufficient possessions to make a good life possible.

In the sixties, however, the backdrop had changed dramatically, from economic insecurity to one of unprecedented prosperity. The sixties were fat city for American middle class, and their children came of age never lacking for what would have been incredible luxuries for their parents. This was Brown's generation, a generation that never wanted for anything money can buy. But you always tend to want whatever it is you don't happen to have, and in their life-styles the sixties generation seemed to be searching for something that they knew money couldn'tbuy. And this is what Brown's life-style seems to represent—something beyond that which can be bought with money.

The way Brown says what he says is also extremely important. He is brusque, sharp, and seems never to equivocate. When running in the 1976 primaries, he was asked what his qualifications for making foreign policy were. His answer: "Clarity of thought." On another occasion, he had this to say about the thrust of his administration. "People ask me, 'What's your program?' What the hell does that mean? The program is to confront the confusion and hypocrisy of government. That's what's important."

Conservatives, wounded by a succession of leaders whose rhetoric was elaborately constructed to mislead, tend to find this apparent directness and bluntness reassuring. And the sixties constituency demands it. They listened to the rhetoric of their Administrations and the leaders of the government that seemed to be at war with them, and they heard pure cant. Today, as many politicians have discovered, they will simply not listen to a traditional political speech. And that is not what Brown gives them.

Brown also knows how not to talk to his sixties constituency and what not to talk to them about. For one thing, you don't talk about what the press and the traditional politicians insist on calling the "issues," and you don't talk as if you've got all the answers. Take the matter of prison reform, for instance. Every politician in the country has a standard statement on prisons, all of them exactly like every other, the only differences being the ideological coloration of the politician involved. If liberal, he will lay out the standard line about "rehabilitation"; if conservative he'll talk about getting criminals off the street; and if moderate there'll be a bit of both. Brown, however, addresses the issue this way: "Prisons don't rehabilitate, they don't punish, they don't protect, so what the hell do they do?"

That sort of thing deeply annoys political traditionalists, who like to define what the issues are and expect the appropriate stand to be taken on them in the appropriate trite and tried language. But that is not what Brown's special sixties constituency is interested in. Most of those things we call "issues," things like the Panama Canal, for instance, they believe are not "issues" at all, but rather superficial controversies manufactured by power-hungry politicians attempting to mobilize a constituency, and adopted as "issues" by the press, which understands little about what people really think, in order to make their job of pigeonholing and categorizing easier. Thus, Brown will increasingly come to be labeled "superficial" by the establishment press as his exposure widens and he continues to refuse to talk about the "issues" in the way he is supposed to. But Brown, of course, won't be terribly put out by that, for he isn't talking to the press.

This is not to say that there are not plenty of things pecking away at the body politic that can legitimately be called "issues." There are, in abundance. But the issues of today are totally different from the issues of the past decade. The old social issues will be whipped up by conservatives at least one or two more times, and the liberals will play their own empty tunes, identifying "issues" that became moribund a decade ago. There will also be the manufactured issues, like the Panama Canal, as well as the serious and significant old issues such as national defense and the economy. But the next time around, most likely in the presidential primary campaign of 1980, the new issues will be pushed center stage by Jerry Brown. These issues—energy and water, for instance—are directly related to the quality of our individual lives and to the quality of the life of our nation as a whole. They are, in effect, cultural issues. Among Brown's special sixties constituency, these are already the trendy issues, and for the rest of the nation, they will eventually become central. And for Brown himself, they may be the issues on which he rides into the White House.

During my last visit to California, I watched Brown play the politics of water, a potentially powerful weapon sure to be used against Jimmy Carter in the western primaries in 1980. It was in November 1977, the last days of the great drought, when the Sunbelt seemed on the verge of turning permanently into the Droughtbelt. The drought had killed 18 million trees in less than a year, more than had been destroyed in California by forest fires. At the airports and in public facilities, signs warned us not to flush unnecessarily. People had given up washing their cars, and the beautiful semitropical foliage and the home gardens of northern California had turned brown. Against this backdrop, Californians had become extremely water conscious, and suddenly, in California as in much of the West, the politics of water had become central, with profound national implications. The California drought is over now, but Californians have been sensitized to the water issue. And throughout the West, especially in the Southwest, water is well on its way to becoming the number one issue. In cities like Pheonix, for instance, where the ground-water table is dropping with dizzying speed, the talk is being revived of somehow diverting the waters of the Columbia River to the Southwest, something that does not make Northwesterners happy. But the situation in Pheonix, which depends heavily on the Colorado River for its irrigation, is approaching the desperate. The rest of the Southwest—and especially southern California—also depends heavily on the Colorado River. And the fear is that the Colorado just won't carry enough water to go around as we approach the next century. The stakes are high, and Jimmy Carter, whose water politics have already alienated much of the West, stands to be the big loser. And in California and much of the rest of the West, the winner may be Jerry Brown.

Each week of 1977 brought another jolt to water conscious Californians, and in each case, rightly or wrongly, the villain of the piece was the federal government. In November, for instance, the U. S. Bureau of Reclamation, which during normal times supplies irrigation water for 2 million acres of farmland in the Sacramento and San Joaquin valleys, announced out of the blue that it just might cut off all federal water supplies entirely in January. In this case, of course, the villain was the drought. But the feds were carrying the message, and as a result there was a good deal of muttering about mismanagement and the whole somewhat peculiar concept of "federal water." At what point, one sometimes wonders does a raindrop become U. S. government property?

But no matter. The federal government can't be blamed for the drought. But there are other cases in which the government in general and the Carter administration in particular are clearly at fault. There was, for instance, the horrendously timed proposal, made by the Interior Department at the height of the drought to break up all farms irrigated by "federal water" into 160-acre, homestead-sized tracts. The ostensible purpose of the breakup, according to Interior Secretary Cecil Andrus, was to encourage "family farming." But in places like the Imperial Valley, one of most important two-crop agricultural areas in the United States, growers already operate family farms—but family farms of considerably more than 160 acres.

The implications of such federal schemes are enormous, touching not only the economy of California but the nation, and threatening the stability of our supply of farm produce to boot. The basic issue involved may not strictly be a water issue. But because water use is central to the Administration's proposal, water-sensitized Westerners tend to see it as part of the whole water problem, and Jerry Brown is playing it for all it's worth, in the process sending Administration officials up the wall. Brown, who once seemed to favor the breakup, now maintains he is dead against a "broad brush approach," and favors only a trial of the proposal in a limited area. Administration officials, however, insist that Brown was enthusiastic about the idea until the political liabilities became clear. In fact, the feds were so incensed at Brown's apparent shift last autumn, that Cecil Andrus, in an interview with the *Sacramento Bee*, took the unusual step of attacking Brown in his own state, charging his alleged shift on the breakup issue was yet another example of "weathervane politics."

Many of Brown's California critics agree, believing that Brown intentionally led the Administration on, then reversed his position, leaving Carter out on the limb all by himself, and looking even worse in California and much of the West than he looked before water was whipped up into a primary political issue. But no matter. The repeated bumbling of the Administration in dealing with the West is so obtrusive that most Westerners now refer routinely to the Administration's "War Against the West." And the apparent inability of the Administration to understand the West's unique problems is a strong argument for Brown's insistence on regional management rather than remote and wrong-headed management from Washington. Were he to become President, Brown's enthusiasm for decentralization might noticeably diminish. But for the present, it is a poweful issue that cuts across established ideological lines. Traditional conservatives have long advocated decentralization as as panacea for regional problems. And the sixties constituency, with its strong emphasis on community control and participatory democracy, sees in a revived regionalism a defense against the depredations of an insensitive and power-hungry alien central government in Washington. Water is a quality-of-life issue with ideological implications, and among Brown's special constituency, it is part of the larger cultural issue to which they believe Brown speaks.

It is no simple task to hold the frequently dissimilar and opposing strands of his support together, and this no doubt accounts for what his critics view as Brown's shiftiness on previously stated positions. Much is being made, for instance, of his turnaround on the limits-to-growth philosophy. At first he seemed intent on holding down business expansion in the state; now he is encouraging it. But the sorts of businesses he seems to be attempting to attract are high-technology rather than basic-goods manufacturing industries. Unlike most utopia among the sixties generation, he seems to understand that his state cannot survive without the revenue and jobs created by business. But at the same time, with the emphasis on clean, high-technology industries, he does nothing to threaten the quality of life. Further, his approach may be just the approach of the future. In many of the basic manufacturing industries, we have already priced ourselves out of the international market because of inefficiency, high labor costs, and our federally encouraged shortage of resources. Thus Brown, whose state is already a major Asian trading partner, believes that the future lies in developing and exporting what we do best. We can export the products of America's unique technological genius to the rest of the world, and our trading partners will provide us with the basic goods produced by manufacturing economies.

Inevitably, Brown must make trade-offs, as any politician must do, and this perhaps accounts for what conservative critics believe to be one of his most shortsighted decisions, the apparent decision to jettison the development of nuclear power. Eventually the critics say, the world will run out of its supply of hydrocarbons. When the oil is gone, it will be necessary to have some alternative power source in place, And nuclear power—safe, clean, and ultimately inexpensive—they believe, should be that source. And for a time, it seemed it would. California, not too long ago, was slated to become the nation's nuclear power showplace. But at this writing, one plant near San Francisco has been closed, and of the remaining two in operation, the plant near Sacramento is in trouble. Furthermore, the California Energy Resources Conservation and Development Commission, which must approve any new nuclear plant construction and is packed with Brown appointees, has just turned thumbs down on plans for a plant in the South, and unless the legislature pushes on, Californians believe this spells the death knell for nuclear development in California. Says Huey Johnson, Jerry Brown's energy adviser: "Nuclear power shouldn't have anything to do with our destiny." And apparently it won't.

This may be shortsighted. But it may also be inevitable, given the nature of Brown's special sixties constituency and their central role in the life and politics of California. Throughout the state, and especially in the north, nuclear energy has become an emotional and cultural issue, one of the few that clearly harks back to the great causes of the sixties. During my last visit to California, for instance, at a "teach-in" in Berkeley, there was Barry Commoner, singing of the utopia society we can create with "soft" sources. And at the same meeting, there was Daniel Ellsberg, inveighing against the neutron bomb, adding the emotional and symbolic dimension to the debate—as if somehow a nuclear generating plant is the same thing as a neutron bomb. Once again, this time on the nuclear power issue, it's hawks versus doves. And once again, although they are outnumbered, the doves dominate the campuses and the news media. And so, in California, the wave of the energy future may be sunshine and windmills. Brown has little choice: His special constituency will go along with technological development, as long as it is clean. But they draw the line at nuclear development, for the very word nuclear touches something deep within them, planted during the upheavals of the sixties. And perhaps it's just as well, for at some point we're going to have to make a serious commitment to developing solar energy, and California may be the place.

Brown, more than any other presidential aspirant, has an eye fixed firmly on the issues of the future, and seems to understand the cultural as well as the economic nature of these issues. His critics heaped great scorn on him for having included $5.5 million in his budget for a California-run space program, the first step of which would be the building of a communications satellite. The idea of a single state having its own space program boggles minds in Washington. But in Washington minds are easily boggled at any sign of imagination and independence, and someone eventually has to do something to build on our achievements in space. If the earth's resources are being depleted and its population continues to multiply, then we will eventually have to expand in order to find more resources and create new living space. And all futurists agree that space is the ultimate answer. Bogged down as we are by the tired old issues that are never solved and yearly grow worse—urban blight, for instance, welfare, the energy crisis—it requires a certain leap of imagination to see ahead to man's great leap into space. But just a few years back, it also took a great leap of imagination to conceive of men walking on the moon. There are always great gaps in such ventures. More than a century passed between the day Columbus sighted the New World and the *Mayflower* sailed. But eventually, it did sail, just as eventually man will mount massive journeys into space. And where better to begin than in California, the land of the future that boasts the lion's share of our Nobel Prize winners?

And it is, perhaps, essential that we begin soon. We sorely lack the unifying cause and vision that in the past accounted for our great technological surges and our unprecedented standard of living. But today there is no such cause and no such vision. Once a war would have done it for us, but that was a simpler day, and the rising generation will have nothing to do with war. Were our leaders to propose another one to us, one suspects they'd have to fight it themselves. Nor is there sufficient romance and meaning in the Peace Corps, urban renewal, or revenue sharing to fire the nation's imagination. there is only one answer, and that answer is space.

Brown, of course, is accused of capitalizing on such cultural phenomena as the success of *Star Wars* and *Close Encounters of the Third Kind*. And no doubt he is. But there is nothing wrong with the men we pay to lead us being in tune with the temper of the times, and perhaps we should be grateful that at least one of them realizes that something different is stirring out there that transcends the mundane old "issues" of the day. In fact, given a vision sufficiently broad to fire the imagination of a new generation, all those "issues" might just disappear. Nor is there any special discrepancy between a limits-to-growth policy here on earth and an expansion into space. That expansion, after all, if successful, would automatically solve the problems that make a consideration of such a policy seem necessary.

According to Richard Reeves, Eugene McCarthy chided Brown about his space program and suggested he concentrate on "the real things down here." Replied Brown: "Space is the future. It is exploration—new world, new ideas, new solutions—the possibilities are limitless. What do you think Queen Isabella was doing when she told Columbus to sail? You think she was just being an escapist?"

Does Brown represent the liberal-conservative-new- politics-sixties generation wave of the future? One suspects he just may, and if it isn't Brown, then it will be someone very much like him. The powerful old liberal wing of the Democratic party seems to have died with Hubert Humphrey, the quintessential New Deal politician, and the Republican-Conservatives and Conservative-Republicans seem more interested in battling one another to extinction than in governing the nation. Where does that leave Carter? Perhaps only students of the Bible and born-again believers can tell us that. But in the meantime, Jerry Brown has his eye on Carter's job, and at the moment the most significant political contest of the past three decades may take place in the Democratic primaries of 1980. A good deal may depend on whether the Democratic National Committee accepts the recommendations of the Winograd Commission that the primary season be telescoped into three months, and whether the states agree to the abridgment. A shorter season might prevent the bandwagon effect an insurgent candidacy can develop from January to June, and minimize the sort of damage Reagan did to Ford over half a year.

Nevertheless, Winograd recommendations or no, few Californians doubt that Brown will take Carter on. Thanks to Administration insensitivity to the new cultural issues, Brown stands a chance of sweeping every Western primary, and he has strong pockets of support in the Northeast and in Middle Atlantic states such as Maryland, which he took in 1976. A few years back, the idea of an insurgent unseating an incumbent in the primaries was unheard of. But that was before the decade of the sixties, when nearly everything previously unheard of took place at least once.

And should Brown not unhorse Carter in 1980, he still has plenty of time. He is sure at the very least to make a strong showing in the primaries, although some of the expected candidacies—that of Senator Moynihan, for instance—may deny him the Northeast. Nevertheless, his showing will be sufficiently strong to position him for an all-out run in 1984. First, reelection in November. Then, in 1980, the primaries, in which Brown will at worst do well and at best spectacularly, insuring he remains a national figure with a demonstrated broad-based popular appeal. In 1982 he will attempt to take Hayakawa's seat in a race that, if it takes place, should tell us a good deal more about Brown's constituency and his appeal to conservatives. And then, in 1984, it will be the Democratic presidential nomination. (This book was written before Proposition 13. But Brown quickly made that issue his own, pointing out, with some plausibility, that it is a natural outgrowth of his philosophy of limits. And it has done no apparent damage to his prospects.)

Given the nature of recent political history, long-range scenarios have a way of turning out totally wrong. But if nothing terrible happens over the next two years, if no one resigns or is impeached or steps aboard a UFO and disappears forever, then the elections of 1980 should tell us a great deal about the new context that seems to be developing out of the ashes of the past decade. Liberals? Conservatives? New Right? Perhaps. But one suspects that the old terms don't really have much to do with it all any longer, and the next clash may be cultural rather than ideological, morality versus consciousness, Hellenism versus Hebraism, and perhaps, if Carter and Brown do slug it out, Ezekiel's Wheel versus Spaceship Earth.

CHAPTER TEN

CALIFORNIA, our only nation-state, is a place of endings and beginnings, and in California's present we frequently see most clearly our future and our past. This is especially true of politics, and in 1976 in California, for the first time, many of the men who personify our political past, present, and future appeared together on the same stage.

There was Morris Udall and Frank Church, representing the best of the old liberalism that officially died with Hubert Humphrey, gliding through the state almost unnoticed, pursuing the presidential nomination for which, as men out of their own time, they had no chance.

There was Senator John Tunney, who managed to salvage renomination only because of the edge his incumbency gave him, flitting from stop to stop like a slightly defective Kennedy, a faint echo from an almost forgotten Camelot, and all it had briefly come to represent.

There was Robert Finch, former Nixon protégé and cabinet member, plodding after the Republican senatorial nomination, wearing navy-blue suits and American flag lapel pins, looking more like Richard Nixon every year. "I've always been proud of the fact that I'm an institutional Republican," he insisted on telling his audiences, and they looked at him as if he were speaking an arcane and nearly incomprehensible tongue.

You *are* Socialists, I asked? Oh yes, they told me, and sold me a copy of their newspaper, *New Solidarity*, and a magazine called *Fusion*, which laid out, in response to "the no-energy program of the Administration," a U. S. Labor party energy program that would make the chairman of the board of Exxon smile. There was a little hedging on natural-gas prices, to be sure. They are, after all, *Socialists*. But the program adamantly opposed funds for developing "soft" energy sources, and it was full speed ahead on "exploitation of existing [oil] wells and further exploration." Strange.

On the plane to California, I looked at their paper. The hero of the day, his picture prominently displayed on the front page, was Richard Nixon's old chum, Teamsters' boss Frank Fitzsimmons. And inside, singled out for praise for his "statesmanlike rallying of the American population" on the energy issue, was the man Richard Nixon really wanted for Vice-President—John Connally. Odd. Also in the same issue, there was a reference to activity by "every Fabian ideologue from the Ford Foundation's McGeorge Bundy to the *National Review*." Had anyone, I wondered, ever called Buckley's *National Review that* before?

And finally, just to ice the martini, there was an ad running in their magazine for the Conservative Book Club, an adjunct operation of Arlington House, the most venerable of the surviving Old Right publishing companies. At that point it was back to *Newsweek*. Obviously they were right. If *National Review* is a hotbed of Fabianism, then Gary Hart and Jerry Brown are certainly conservatives.

And perhaps, according to who defines the term and how, they are, for things have shifted radically during the past decade, and the old terms, which we once wore into battle, frequently seem as meaningless as last year's campaign speeches. Not long ago, at a birthday dinner, my two oldest children, Jennifer and John, were asking questions about politics, a topic I have seldom discussed with them. The subject had something to do with the governmental desire to regulate, and I was trying to explain to them what I understood the conservative and liberal positions to be. The liberals, I said, believed we were unable to care for ourselves and wanted to regulate everything in sight. On the other hand, I said, conservatives believed that people should be as free from regulation as possible. They looked puzzled. *We* thought, they told me, that it was just the other way around. And perhaps it is.

All in all, a marvelous decade. I also remember a shopping trip that my wife described to me. She was scouring a secondhand furniture store, as she likes to do, and came across an old photograph of Hitler strolling with his High Command. My youngest daughter, Charity, who knows I worked for Mr. Agnew and Mr. Nixon, as she calls them, looked thoughtfully at the picture of Hitler. "Mom," she asked seriously, "did Daddy work for that man too?"

Not him, Charity. But a couple of other rather peculiar gentlemen. And what was it all about? I'm not sure. I can lay it out on paper—Berkeley, the New Left, the breakdown of order and civility, the counterrevolution, victory, the collapse. We were necessary, I think, for certain things had to be halted, and there had to be a final confrontation to clear the air of a decade's worth of high emotional detritus. Did we succeed? I believe we did. We succeeded by losing, and by doing so we helped bring to an end an era that had to be ended. Perhaps Jimmy Carter and those who follow him will prove incapable of building a new synthesis. But we made it possible, and if they fail, it will be in no way our fault.

Nor will it be likely to have much to do with us if they succeed. In many ways, we were the last gasp of a political generation for which the battle lines had been drawn up during the days of the New Deal. American political history from the forties to the mid-seventies is in large part the history of skirmishes between the ideologies that grew out of that period, but now the battles, in the main, are over. Richard Nixon represented the last of the leaders of one camp, and, at least symbolically, Hubert Humphrey the last real leader of the other. But now they are both gone, and today new leaders of only vaguely recognizable movements are mapping out totally new plans for the battles of the future.

Those battles will not be ours, nor will the society that

emerges from them be the sort of society we once thought we were fighting for but in the end helped to destroy when we won by losing. The trend is irreversibly toward some sort of totally controlled society, with Washington inexorably tightening its grip. Perhaps it won't quite be socialism, and it certainly won't be called that, any more than national health insurance, when it finally comes in, will be called socialized medicine. Americans just don't like the sound of the term, with its Eastern European connotations. But it will be something very much like socialism, perhaps a New-World eclectic combination of fascism and social democracy, with segments of the business world retaining nominal control over their operations and serving as corporate managers responsible primarily to government.

This isn't at all farfetched. The health care system, one of the last shrinking bastions of free enterprise practice, will be governmentally directed within our lifetimes. With the creation of the massive new Department of Energy, its budget already at $10.5 billion, an amount larger than the gross earnings of the seventeen largest oil companies, the government has taken the first step in a process that everyone in Washington believes will eventually, and not too many years down the road, lead to a takeover of the energy industries. And after energy, steel, autos, and the rest of them will follow rapidly. And even if it doesn't amount on paper to a total takeover, the combination of taxes and proliferating regulations—about 25,000 new ones each year—will add up to much the same thing.

There will be a few more guerrilla actions aimed at rolling it back. Jerry Brown may get to the White House and may continue there to make decentralization a central issue. But that isn't likely. People tend to change their minds about sharing power once they have it all firmly in their grasp. And it is probable at this writing that Ronald Reagan will once more lead what may be the final charge of the Conservative-Republicans. But the odds against Reagan winning are considerably longer than were the odds against Lee at Gettysburg.

Conservative? Liberal? Agnew? Nixon? That's all over now,

the field is open to the Browns and Harts, and those of us who fought the last political battles of the decade are for the most part burned-out spectators, not even quite sure any longer just what it was all about. I can convincingly—at least to my own satisfaction—chart it all out on paper. But the feelings are gone now, and without the feelings the charts seem little more than that. Were they all really revolutionaries? Were we really counterrevolutionaries? Was the Republic really in danger? I once believed intensely that it was. But now, with the feelings dead, I can't be sure. Perhaps it was something much simpler. A cheer I remember hearing at a University of California football game keeps running through my mind: "Marijuana, marijuana, Ho Chi Minh/ Right on, Golden Bears, cop a win." Was *that* what it was all about?

Perhaps. But I hope not. Surely it took something a great deal more than that to ignite those emotions. But I can no longer find it. I looked for it on that last trip to Berkeley, where it all began for me. For a decade, Berkeley had remained my central point of reference, the place that everything I had become had grown out of. At least once a year I return, and those old feelings would come sweeping back, leaving me with my belief in the rightness of what we were doing reinforced.

But on the last trip, the feelings just weren't there. I revisited all the scenes of the great confrontations—People's Park, now partly a parking lot; Moses Hall, now just another building; the Sproul steps, where the crowds no longer gather to hear the lunchtime speakers; Telegraph Avenue, from which the last wisp of tear gas and the last shard of broken glass had vanished long ago. I walked down Telegraph to the Heidelberg, where I once drank beer and snarled at the street scene outside and wrote twenty supercharged pages at a sitting. But on the last visit two beers were more than I needed and the pages just didn't come. The street scene wasn't that much different from the sixties, and the thought occurred, no doubt belatedly, that what I had been recording in those days was as much internal as external.

Some feelings did return briefly on that last visit. I left the campus and walked the four miles to the married student housing complex where we had lived in the sixties. It was the same old route of a decade ago, and I made all the old crossings and turns automatically, and as I walked I found that I was thinking the same old thoughts and rehearsing the same old debates, now long dead, that had so fired me ten years earlier, just as if they were all still there, hanging in the California air, waiting for me to catch up with them again as I walked. And perhaps they were. If you've existed in a certain place at a certain time, then perhaps something remains there when you leave—an idea, perhaps, or a feeling, flimsy as a cobweb, but nevertheless there.

The old route took me to the housing complex, and as I turned the corner I could see the green door on the second-floor barracks apartment where we had lived, and for a moment I could see my daughter Amanda, in a pink dress, waiting for me to return from campus, just as she had a decade ago. There was a little flash somewhere inside, a blink, and for a second I was coming home again. But then, just as rapidly, it was gone. On the window of the room in which I wrote my first pieces for *National Review* there was a poster with a women's rights slogan emblazoned on it. Nothing of us there at all. Around back, however, was a trace. There on the black mailbox a small bit of masking tape still clung, a piece of the strip upon which I had written our names ten years ago. And that was it. Not much, but it was something.

We had been very happy there, in that married student apartment in Berkeley. I was perpetually angry at what I saw each day on the campus, and I came home angry each evening to write, and that anger helped make us very happy. It was, no doubt, overreaction. But we were a very happy family, and what was happening at Berkeley a decade ago seemed to have a direct bearing on the sort of world my children could expect to grow up in. "We're going to get your kids," Abbie Hoffman and Jerry Rubin used to say. And they did get a lot of them. But not my kids. Somehow, although I know it was all very dangerous, that seems a bit amusing these days. In the sixties, convinced it was all part of the counterculture politicizing process, I attacked in print the music of groups such as the Rolling Stones and the Grateful Dead, and vowed that my children would never be seduced by that music. Today, however, my teenage son plays Grateful Dead tapes, they sound perfectly harmless compared to much of the evil music of the newest generation, and I am thankful that he scorns the new punk abominations.

In the end, I realized on that last trip, it had been a very personal thing. We were very happy, we were very innocent, and perhaps we retained that innocence, in fact fought to retain it, until the day we learned that Spiro Agnew, protector of the American family and its values and symbol of our fight, was one more petty politico on the take, and that Richard Nixon, after all, was just Richard Nixon.

But no matter, I had found my piece of masking tape, all that was left of the life we had lived there, and I doubt that I will ever go back. Perhaps what I was looking for was a fierce and happy innocence, and innocence was made to be lost. We are still happy, and the children have grown up, despite all the odds against them, very straight and very clean. Nevertheless, although I suppose we are happier than most of our married contemporaries, there is still that bit of masking tape, all that's left of the innocence we lost and the way we were.

I walked back to the Berkeley campus on that visit for the last time. Everyone there still seemed as young and energetic and even as innocent as ever, no matter what their ages. Perhaps Berkeley is by definition the quintessentially innocent place, a place of beginnings, with everyone who journeys there starting from scratch, a place to which people from across the country travel to begin again and make new discoveries. And perhaps that's why I can't recapture those old feelings. There are still touches, still twinges, still that wash of nostalgia that makes the eyes blur. But there's a problem: I no longer have a place there, for I've finished my own trip.

And so, a decade later, that's that. I took a flight back that also stopped at O'Hare, and spent the better part of an evening there. I was careful to dodge my friends near the TWA counter, still out in force. No doubt they were sincere in doing what they were doing, and no doubt they represented something that all writers with an interest in politics should attempt to plumb. But they're part of something new, which has nothing to do with me, and I had stopped at O'Hare to say some good-bys and toast a few old friends and enemies.

O'Hare's Seven Continents bar, where I first stopped a bit more than a decade ago on the first trip to Berkeley, is the proper place to do it, in part because O'Hare is a crossroads stop, the halfway point for many serious travelers, and conditions are just about perfect at the halfway point, especially if you've just left a good flight. You're *in* the damned thing, everything has been ripped from your hands, you're *responsible* for nothing, and you *taste* your drinks and you *taste* your cigarettes, as you haven't tasted them for years, and all those things you've filed away in the back of your mind—the good and happy things and the unhappy things as well—come rushing back.

That's how it is at O'Hare. You're right in the middle. You're in between flights and the best part is still ahead. Later, of course, it ends, for the price you pay as a solitary traveler is getting there. But at O'Hare you're in between, and for that brief moment you space things out, and once again there's plenty of time. In what we call the real world, framed in the minutes of our daily lives, real time does grow shorter. But we learn to live for the pauses, during which we stretch time out so that the possibilities that seemed so real a decade or so ago seem as real as ever. And when the place is just right and the talk is right, there's just as much time as there used to be. And for the duration of that pause, it's nice to think so.

And so, a bit more than ten years after I had first paused at O'Hare on my way to Berkeley, a few toasts with Beck's beer to that lost decade. Here's to masking tape, marijuana, Ho Chi Minh. Here's to Mario Savio, Bettina Apetheker, Jerry Rubin, Abbie Hoffman, Timothy Leary, Ché Guevara, Mao and Chou, Joan Baez, the Rolling Stones, the Grateful Dead, John and Bobby, Mary Jo, both K. and B., Martin Luther King, LBJ, Clark Kerr, Herbert Marcuse, Huey Newton, Eldridge Cleaver, Charles Manson, Squeaky and Ouisch, Bernadine Dohrn, Mark Rudd, Max Rafferty, Lester Maddox, Mayor Daley, Ved Nanda, Charlie Schaefer, the veteran Max McGee, Haldeman, Ehrlichman, Mitchell, Nixon, Spiro Agnew. Their like will never pass this way again.

Here's to folk rock, hard rock, the Hell's Angels, Altamont, Janis Joplin, Mamma Cass, Grandma Schaefer, the Pentagon Papers, Chicago, People's Park, Stop the Draft Week, the New Mobe, Kent State, impudent snobs, nattering nabobs of negativism, Cambodia Spring, the SDS, the YSA, Haiphong Harbor, the dikes, the Parrot's beak, B-52's, defoliation, sensors, secure Hamlets, the lift of a driving dream, the lasting structure of peace, the eighteen-and-a-half-minute gap, the Sinister Force, the Reverend Moon, Rabbi Korff, Father John, Palm Springs, the western White House, Dan Rather, the Florida White House, black studies, *Deep Throat*, the miniskirt, burning bras, women's lib, Germaine Greer, Helen Clark, McSorley's Tavern, Hare Krishna, Madame Nhu, Big Minh, Henry Cabot Lodge, Youth for Nixon, "My Kind of Guy, Ted Agnew is", I will not resign if indicted, I am not a crook, Four More Years, you destroy yourself.

Here's to the good guys—William Buckley, James Buckley, Priscilla Buckley, Daniel Patrick Moynihan, Eugene McCarthy, Claus Naske, S. I. Hayakawa, Herman Slotnick, Chuck Keim, Bill Magee, Minnie Wells, Orlando Miller, Arthur Wills, Dean Rusk, Norman Thomas, Erich Hoffer, Stewart Alsop, Vince Lombardi, George Allen, R. Emmett Tyrrell, The Baron, Gergen, Koch, Morgan, Barbieri, Buchanan, Khachigian, Bakshian, and Ben Stein, founder of hippies, heads, and starlets for Nixon.

Here's to the Old Left, the New Left, the Old Liberalism, the Old Conservatism, the New Right, the New New Right, the New New New Right, Here's to morality and consciousness, to Bible Study and Zen Jogging, to Hellenism and Hebraism, to born-again believers and Jerry Brown's Hobbit constituency.

Here's to the Queen of the Matanuska Valley State Fair, the girl with the most beautiful eyes in Alaska, who staggered along with me through the decade. And here's to Jennife John, Amanda, and Charity, each of them a child of the sixtie and all them champion children. They didn't get them, afte all. They never even came close.

Here's to Berkeley, where the decade began for so many o us, and to Washington, where it so abruptly ended.

And finally, here's to the end of the trip, here's to innocence, here's to nostalgia, and here's to all of us and the way we thought we were.